BLACK & DECKER®

OUTDOOR HOME™

Outdoor
WOOD FURNISHINGS

CREATIVE PUBLISHING international

MINNETONKA, MINNESOTA

www.howtobookstore.com

Credits

Executive Editor: Bryan Trandem
Associate Creative Director: Tim Himsel
Managing Editor: Jennifer Caliandro
Lead Editor: Daniel London
Editors: Clayton Bennett, Nora Leven,
  D. R. Martin, Susan Wichmann
Technical Editors: Philip Schmidt,
  Richard Steven
Copy Editor: Janice Cauley
Mac Designers: Patti Goar, Jonathan Hinz,
  Jon Simpson, Brad Webster

Vice President of Photography & Production:
  Jim Bindas
Studio Services Manager: Marcia Chambers
Photo Services Coordinator: Carol Osterhus
Photo Team Leader: Chuck Nields
Cover Photographer: John Lauenstein
Scene Shop Carpenters: Troy Johnson,
  Dan Widerski
Production Manager: Kim Gerber

CREATIVE
PUBLISHING
international

Copyright© 1999
Creative Publishing international, Inc.
5900 Green Oak Drive
Minnetonka, MN 55343
1-800-328-3895
www.howtobookstore.com
All rights reserved
Printed on American Paper by:
  R.R. Donnelley & Sons Co.
10 9 8 7 6 5 4 3 2

President/CEO: David D. Murphy
Vice President/Editorial: Patricia K. Jacobsen
Vice President/Retail Sales & Marketing:
  Richard M. Miller

OUTDOOR WOOD FURNISHINGS
Created by: The Editors of Creative
Publishing international, Inc. in coopera-
tion with Black & Decker. Black & Decker
is a trademark of the Black & Decker
Corporation and is used under license.

Library of Congress
Cataloging-in-Publication Data

Outdoor wood furnishings :
35 easy projects for your yard.

p. cm. — (Black & Decker outdoor home)
Includes index.
ISBN 0-86573-633-2 (softcover)
1. Outdoor furniture--Design and construction. 2. Garden ornaments and furniture--
Design and construction. 3. Woodwork. 4.
Power tools. I. Creative Publishing International. II. Series. TT197.5.O9o9825
1998
684.1'8--DC21   98-49168

Contents

Introduction

Outdoor furnishings have the remarkable ability to transform your porch, patio or deck into a beckoning space. And no material does this more effectively than wood. Adding a tree surround or Adirondack chair to your yard or a trellis planter to your garden can transform even the simplest spaces. Whether you enjoy unfettered relaxation in the backyard, or down-and-dirty work in the garden, affordable, yet visually pleasing, furnishings will help you get the most out of your time outdoors. A quick glance through *Outdoor Wood Furnishings* reveals attractive planters, a simple-to-build bird feeder stand, as well as workhorse items like a yard-and-garden cart that's so attractive, you'll be tempted to leave it outside all the time. The projects contained in this book make life a little easier for anyone who enjoys the outdoors. Best of all, they are designed for simplicity—you don't need to be an accomplished woodworker to get impressive results.

Outdoor Wood Furnishings is a book of woodworking plans offering you detailed, step-by-step instructions, color photographs, complete cutting and shopping lists and precise construction drawings for each of the 35 projects for your yard, garden, porch, patio and deck. From a handsome mailbox to an enchanting freestanding arbor, you'll be guided through these projects every step of the way.

With *Outdoor Wood Furnishings*, you don't need to be an expert with power tools to create useful, attractive projects. Every item in the book is designed to be built with basic, affordable hand tools and portable power tools that you probably already own.

Outdoor Wood Furnishings gives weekend do-it-yourselfers the ability to take on great projects for outdoor use without spending a lot of money on lumber or investing heavily in power equipment. Ask your local bookseller to show you other books of home do-it-yourself projects from Black & Decker.

NOTICE TO READERS

This book provides useful instructions, but we cannot anticipate all of your working conditions or the characteristics of your materials and tools. For safety, you should use caution, care, and good judgment when following the procedures described in this book. Consider your own skill level and the instructions and safety precautions associated with the various tools and materials shown. Neither the publisher nor Black & Decker® can assume responsibility for any damage to property, injury to persons, or losses incurred as a result of misuse of the information provided.

Organizing Your Work Site

Portable power tools and hand tools offer a level of convenience that is a great advantage over stationary power tools. But using them safely and conveniently requires some basic housekeeping. Whether you are working in a garage or basement or outdoors, it is important that you establish a flat, dry holding area where you can store tools. Set aside a piece of plywood on sawhorses, or dedicate an area of your workbench for tool storage, and be sure to return tools to that area once you are finished with them. It is also important that all waste, including lumber scraps and sawdust, be disposed of in a timely fashion. Check with your local waste disposal department before throwing away large scraps of building materials or finishing-material containers.

> ### Safety Tips
> •*Always wear eye and hearing protection when operating power tools and performing any other dangerous activities.*
> •*Choose a well-ventilated work area when cutting or shaping wood and when using finishing products.*

Tools & Materials

At the start of each project, you will find a set of symbols that show which power tools are used to complete the project as it is shown (see below). You will also need a set of basic hand tools: a hammer, screwdrivers, tape measure, level, combination square, C-clamps, and pipe or bar clamps. Each project includes a shopping list that includes all the construction materials you will need. Miscellaneous materials and hardware are listed with the cutting list that accompanies the construction drawing. When buying lumber, note that the "nominal" size of the lumber is usually larger than the "actual" size. For example, a milled 2 × 4 is actually 1½" × 3½".

Power Tools You Will Use

Circular saw *to make straight cuts. For long cuts and rip-cuts, use a straight-edge guide. Install a carbide-tipped combination blade for most projects.*

Drills: *use a cordless drill for drilling pilot holes and counterbores, and to drive screws; use an electric drill for sanding and grinding tasks.*

Jig saw *for making contoured cuts and internal cuts. Use a combination wood blade for most projects where you will cut pine, cedar or plywood.*

Power sander *to prepare wood for a finish and to smooth out sharp edges. Owning several power sanders (½-sheet, ¼-sheet, and belt) is helpful.*

Belt sander *for resurfacing rough wood. Can also be used as a stationary sander when mounted on its side on a flat work surface.*

Router *to cut decorative edges and roundovers in wood. As you gain more experience, use routers for cutting grooves (like dadoes) to form joints.*

Guide to Major Building Materials and Their Costs

•*Sheet goods:*
PLYWOOD: *Basic sheet good sold in several grades (from CDX to AB) and thicknesses. Inexpensive to moderately expensive.*
CEMENTBOARD: *Heavy cement-based panels often used for floor and wall tile installations. Moderately inexpensive.*
HOUSE SIDING: *Grooved, cedar- or fir-based exterior plywood material. Moderately inexpensive.*
CEDAR LATTICE PANELS: *Prefabricated lattice sheets sold in thickness of ½" to 1". Inexpensive to moderately expensive.*

•*Dimension lumber:*
PINE: *A basic softwood used for many interior projects. "Select" and "#2 or better" are suitable grades. Moderately inexpensive.*
CEDAR: *Excellent outdoor lumber with rich color. Usually sanded on one side and rough on the other. Moderately inexpensive. Available in ⅞" and ¾" thicknesses, depending on the type of board Make sure to purchase the right thickness for your project.*
CEDAR SIDING: *Beveled lap siding. Moderately inexpensive.*

Guide to Fasteners & Adhesives Used in This Book

•*Fasteners & hardware:*
WOOD SCREWS: *Brass or steel; most projects use screws with a #6 or #8 shank. Can be driven with a power driver.*
DECK SCREWS: *Galvanized for weather resistance. Widely spaced threads for good gripping power in soft lumber.*
NAILS & BRADS: *Finish nails can be set below the wood surface: common (box) nails have wide, flat heads; brads or wire nails are very small, thin fasteners with small heads.*
CARRIAGE BOLTS: *Used to secure moving parts. We used ⅜"-dia.*
LAG SCREWS OR BOLTS: *Durable fasteners for extra holding strength.*
MISCELLANEOUS HARDWARE: *10" utility wheels; brass butt hinges; steel axle rod; eye hooks; cotter pins; hitch pins; specialty hardware as indicated.*

•*Adhesives:*
MOISTURE-RESISTANT GLUE: *Any exterior wood glue, such as plastic resin glue.*
EPOXY: *A two-part glue that bonds powerfully and quickly.*

•*Miscellaneous materials:*
Wood plugs (for filling screw counterbores); 1" 22-gauge copper strips; galvanized metal flashing; plexiglass.

Finishing Your Project

Sand all surfaces to remove rough spots and splinters, using medium-grit (120 to 150) sandpaper. Insert wood plugs into screw counterbores and sand until smooth. Fine finish-sanding is usually not necessary for unpainted exterior projects. But you should cover nail and screw heads with wood putty. Then, sand with 180-grit sandpaper if you plan to paint. Most projects in this book are finished with exterior wood stain or clear wood sealer. Look for products that block UV rays, and follow the manufacturer's directions for application. When painting, use exterior primer. Then, apply an enamel or glossy exterior paint.

Garden Bench

Graceful lines and trestle construction make this bench a charming complement to porches, patios and decks—as well as gardens.

CONSTRUCTION MATERIALS

Quantity	Lumber
1	2 × 8" × 6' cedar
4	2 × 2" × 10' cedar
1	2 × 4" × 6' cedar
1	2 × 6" × 10' cedar
1	2 × 2" × 6' cedar
1	1 × 4" × 12' cedar

Casual seating is a welcome addition to any outdoor setting. This lovely garden bench sits neatly at the borders of any porch, patio or deck. It creates a pleasant resting spot for up to three adults without taking up a lot of space. Station it near your home's rear entry and you'll have convenient seating for removing shoes or setting down grocery bags while you unlock the door.

The straightforward design of this bench lends itself to accessorizing. Station a rustic cedar planter next to the bench for a lovely effect. Or, add a framed lattice trellis to one side of the bench to cut down on wind and direct sun.

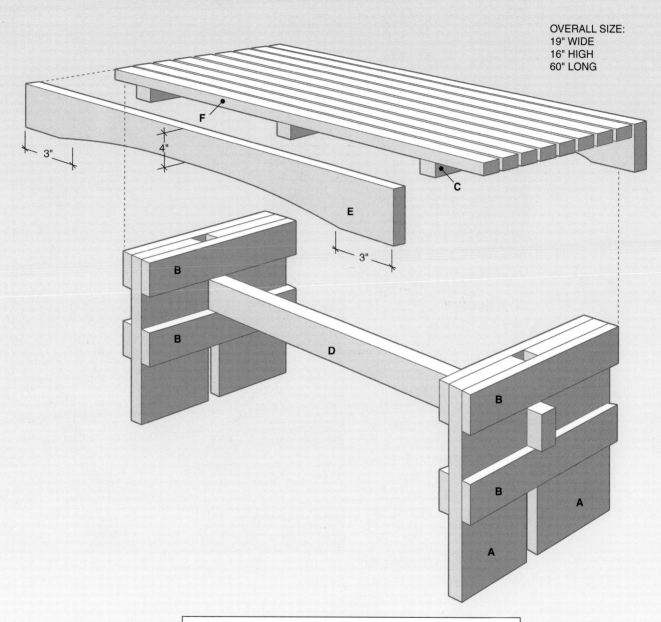

OVERALL SIZE:
19" WIDE
16" HIGH
60" LONG

3"

4"

F

C

E

3"

B

B

D

B

A

B

A

A

Cutting List

Key	Part	Dimension	Pcs.	Material
A	Leg half	1½ × 7¼ × 14½"	4	Cedar
B	Cleat	¾ × 3½ × 16"	8	Cedar
C	Brace	1½ × 1½ × 16"	3	Cedar
D	Trestle	1½ × 3½ × 60"	1	Cedar
E	Apron	1½ × 5½ × 60"	2	Cedar
F	Slat	1½ × 1½ × 60"	8	Cedar

Materials: Moisture-resistant glue, wood sealer or stain, 1½", 2½" deck screws.

Note: Measurements reflect the actual size of dimension lumber.

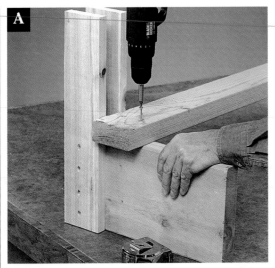

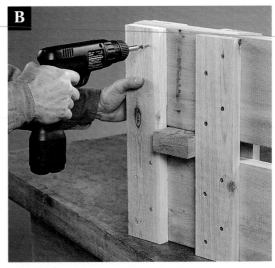

Make sure the trestle is positioned correctly against the cleats, and attach it to the leg.

Attach the remaining leg half to the cleats on both ends to complete the leg assembly.

Directions: Garden Bench

BUILD THE BASE.

1. Cut the leg halves (A), cleats (B) and trestle (D) to length. Sandwich one leg half between two cleats so the cleats are flush with the top and the outside edge of the leg half. Then, join the parts by driving four 1½" deck screws through each cleat and into the leg half. Assemble two more cleats with a leg half in the same fashion.

2. Stand the two assemblies on their sides, with the open ends of the cleats pointing upward. Arrange the assemblies so they are roughly 4' apart. Set the trestle onto the inner edges of the leg halves, pressed flush against the bottoms of the cleats. Adjust the position of the assemblies so the trestle overhangs the leg half by 1½" at each end. Fasten the trestle to each leg half with glue and 2½" deck screws **(photo A).**

Attach the outer brace for the seat slats directly to the inside faces of the cleats.

3. Attach another pair of cleats to each leg half directly below the first pair, positioned so each cleat is snug against the bottom of the trestle.
4. Slide the other leg half between the cleats, keeping the top edge flush with the upper cleats. Join the leg halves with the cleats using glue and 2½" deck screws **(photo B).**
5. Cut the braces (C) to length. Fasten one brace to the inner top cleat on each leg assembly, so the tops are flush **(photo C).**

MAKE THE APRONS.

1. Cut the aprons (E) to length.
2. Lay out the arch onto one apron, starting 3" from each end. The peak of the arch, located over the midpoint of the apron, should be 1½" up from the bottom edge.
3. Draw a smooth, even arch by driving a casing nail at the peak of the arch and one at each of the starting points. Slip a flexible ruler behind the nails at the starting points and in front of the nail at the peak to create a smooth arch. Then,

trace along the inside of the ruler to make a cutting line **(photo D)**.

4. Cut along the line with a jig saw and sand the cut smooth.

5. Trace the profile of the arch onto the other apron and make and sand the cut.

6. Cut the slats (F) to length. Attach a slat to the top, inside edge of each apron with glue and deck screws **(photo E)**.

INSTALL THE APRONS AND SLATS.

1. Apply glue at each end on the bottom sides of the attached slats. Flip the leg and trestle assembly and position it flush with the aprons so that it rests on the glue on the bottoms of the two slats. The aprons should extend 1½" beyond the legs at each end of the bench. Drive 2½" deck screws through the braces and into both slats.

2. Position the middle brace (C) between the aprons, centered end to end on the project. Fasten it to the two side slats with deck screws.

3. Position the six remaining slats on the braces, using ½"-thick spacers to create equal gaps between them. Attach the slats with glue and drive 2½" deck screws up through the braces and into each slat **(photo F)**.

APPLY FINISHING TOUCHES.

Sand the slats smooth with progressively finer sandpaper. Wipe away the sanding residue with a rag dipped in mineral spirits. Let the bench dry. Apply a finish of your choice—a clear wood sealer protects the cedar without altering the color.

TIP

Sometimes our best efforts produce furniture that wobbles because it is not quite level. One old trick for leveling furniture is to set a plastic wading pool on a flat plywood surface that is set to an exact level position with shims. Fill the pool with about ¼" of water. Set the furniture in the pool, then remove it quickly. Mark the tops of the waterlines on the legs, and use them as cutting lines for trimming the legs to level.

D

Use a flexible ruler pinned between casing nails to trace a smooth arch onto the aprons.

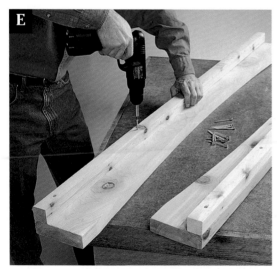

E

Attach a 2 × 2 slat to the top, inside edge of each apron, using 2½" deck screws and glue.

F

Attach the seat slats with glue and 2½" deck screws. Insert ½"-thick spacers to set gaps between the slats.

Picnic Table for Two

Turn a quiet corner of your yard into an intimate setting for dining alfresco with this compact picnic table.

CONSTRUCTION MATERIALS

Quantity	Lumber
1	2 × 8" × 6' cedar
1	2 × 6" × 8' cedar
4	2 × 4" × 8' cedar
3	1 × 6" × 8' cedar
4	1 × 2" × 8' cedar

A picnic table doesn't have to be a clumsy, uncomfortable family feeding trough. In this project, you'll create a unique picnic table that's just the right size for two people to enjoy. Portable and lightweight, it can be set in a corner of your garden, beneath a shade tree or on your deck or patio to enhance your outdoor dining experiences.

The generously proportioned tabletop can be set with full table settings for a formal meal in the garden. But it's intimate enough for sharing a cool beverage with a special person as you watch the sun set. Made with plain dimensional cedar, this picnic table for two is both sturdy and long-lasting.

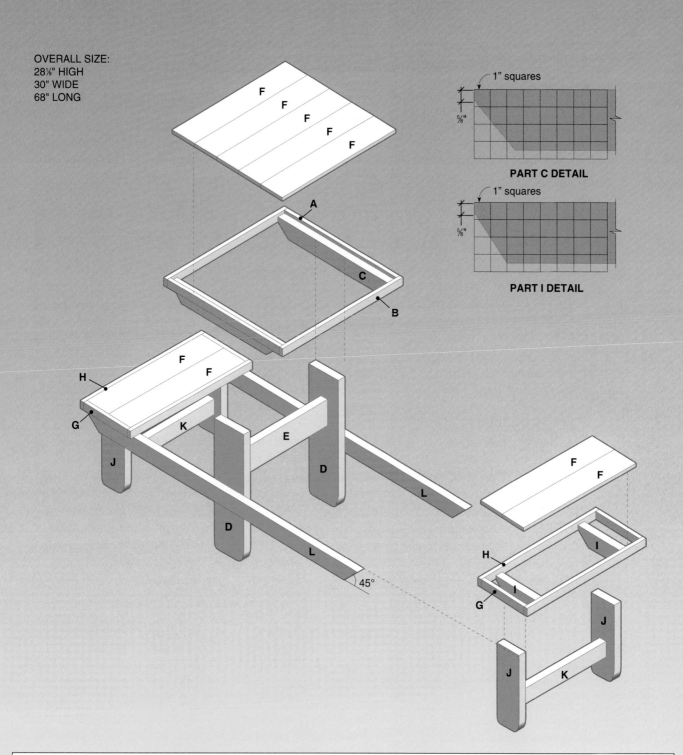

OVERALL SIZE:
28⅛" HIGH
30" WIDE
68" LONG

1" squares
⅝"
PART C DETAIL

1" squares
⅝"
PART I DETAIL

45°

	Cutting List			
Key	**Part**	**Dimension**	**Pcs.**	**Material**
A	Tabletop frame	⅞ × 1½ × 27¾"	2	Cedar
B	Tabletop frame	⅞ × 1½ × 30"	2	Cedar
C	Table stringer	1½ × 3½ × 27¾"	2	Cedar
D	Table leg	1½ × 7¼ × 27¼"	2	Cedar
E	Table stretcher	1½ × 5½ × 22¼"	1	Cedar
F	Slat	⅞ × 5½ × 28¼"	9	Cedar

	Cutting List			
Key	**Part**	**Dimension**	**Pcs.**	**Material**
G	Bench frame	⅞ × 1½ × 11¼"	4	Cedar
H	Bench frame	⅞ × 1½ × 30"	4	Cedar
I	Bench stringer	1½ × 3½ × 11¼"	4	Cedar
J	Bench leg	1½ × 5½ × 15¼"	4	Cedar
K	Bench stretcher	1½ × 3½ × 22¼"	2	Cedar
L	Cross rail	1½ × 3½ × 68"	2	Cedar

Materials: Moisture-resistant glue, 1⅝" and 2½" brass or galvanized deck screws, finishing materials.

Note: Measurements reflect the actual size of dimension lumber.

Make triangular cutoffs at the ends on the table stringers, using a circular saw.

Install the tabletop slats by driving screws through the tabletop frame and into the ends of the slats.

Directions:
Picnic Table for Two

BUILD THE TABLETOP.
1. Cut the tabletop frame pieces (A, B), the table stringers (C) and the table slats (F) to length. Sand the parts.
2. Draw cutting lines that start 2½" from one end of each stringer and connect with a point at the same end, ⅝" in from the opposite edge of the board (see *Diagram*, page 11). Cut along the lines with a circular saw to make the cutoffs **(photo A).**
3. Fasten the shorter tabletop frame pieces (A) to the sides of the stringers. The tops of the frame pieces should extend ⅞" above the tops of the stringers, and the ends should be flush. First, drill ⅛" pilot holes in the frame pieces. Counterbore the holes ¼" deep, using a counterbore bit. Attach the pieces with glue and drive 1⅝" deck screws through the frame pieces and into the stringers.
4. Position the longer tabletop frame pieces (B) so they overlay the ends of the shorter frame pieces. Fasten them to-

gether with glue and 1⅝" deck screws to complete the frames.
5. Set the slats inside the frame so the ends of the slats rest on the stringers. Space the slats evenly. Drill two pilot holes through the tabletop frame by the ends of each slat. Counterbore the holes. Drive 1⅝" deck screws through the frame and into the end of each slat, starting with the two end slats **(photo B).**

MAKE AND ATTACH THE TABLE-LEG ASSEMBLY.
1. Cut the table legs (D) and table stretcher (E) to length. Use a compass to draw a 1½"-radius roundover curve on the corners of one end of each leg. Cut the curves with a jig saw.
2. Hold an end of the stretcher against the inside face of one of the table legs, 16" up from the bottom of the leg and centered side to side. Trace the outline of the stretcher onto the leg. Repeat the procedure on the other leg.
3. Drill two evenly spaced pilot holes through the stretcher outlines on the legs. Counterbore

the holes on the outside faces of the legs. Attach the stretcher with glue and drive 2½" deck screws through the legs and into the ends of the stretcher.
4. Turn the tabletop upside down. Apply glue to the table stringers where they will contact the legs. Position the legs in place within the tabletop frame. Attach them by driving 2½" deck screws through the legs and into the table stringers **(photo C).**

BUILD THE BENCH TOPS.
1. Cut the bench slats (F), bench frame pieces (G, H) and bench stringers (I). Cut the ends of the bench stringers in the same way you cut the table stringers, starting ⅝" from the top edge and 2" from the ends on the bottom edges.
2. Assemble the frame pieces into two rectangular frames by driving 1⅝" deck screws through the longer frame pieces and into the ends of the shorter pieces.
3. Turn the bench frames upside down. Center the bench slats inside them so the outer edges of the slats are flush

Position the table legs inside the tabletop frame, and attach them to the table stringers.

Set the bench legs against the outer faces of the stringers. Attach the legs to the stringers. Then, attach the stretcher between the legs.

against the frame. Attach the slats by driving 1⅝" deck screws through the frames and into the ends of the slats.

4. Fasten the stringers inside the frame so the tops of the stringers are flat against the undersides of the slats, 3" from the inside of each frame end. Attach with glue and drive 1⅝" deck screws through the angled ends of the stringers and into the undersides of the slats. Locate the screws far enough away from the ends of the stringers so they don't stick out through the tops of the slats. The stringers are not attached directly to the bench frames.

BUILD THE BENCH LEGS.
1. Cut the bench legs (J) and bench stretchers (K) to length. With a compass, draw a roundover curve with a 1½" radius on the corners of one end of each leg. Cut the roundovers with a jig saw.
2. Center the tops of the bench legs against the outside faces of the bench stringers. Drill pilot holes in the stringers. Counterbore the holes. Attach the legs to the stringers with glue, and

drive 2½" deck screws through the stringers and into the legs.
3. Drill pilot holes in the bench legs and counterbore the holes in similar fashion to the approach described in "Make and Attach the Table-Leg Assembly," above. Glue the bench stretchers and attach them between the legs with 2½" deck screws **(photo D).**

JOIN THE TABLE
AND BENCHES.
1. Cut the cross rails (L) to length, miter-cutting the ends at a 45° angle (see *Diagram*). Position the benches so the ends of the cross rails are flush with the outside ends of the bench frames. Drill pilot holes in the cross rails. Counterbore the holes. Apply glue and attach the cross rails to the bench legs with 2½" deck screws.

2. Stand the benches up and center the table legs between the cross rails. Apply glue to the joints between the cross rails and legs. Clamp the table legs to the cross rails, making sure the parts are perpendicular **(photo E).** Secure the parts by driving several 2½" deck screws through the cross rails and into the outside face of each leg.

APPLY FINISHING TOUCHES.
Sand all the sharp edges and flat surfaces of the table. Apply a nontoxic wood sealant.

Center the table within the cross rails, and clamp it in place.

Adirondack Chair

You will find dozens of patterns and plans for building popular Adirondack chairs in just about any bookstore, but few are simpler to make or more attractive than this clever project.

Adirondack furniture has become a standard on decks, porches and patios throughout the world. It's no mystery that this distinctive furniture style has become so popular. Attractive—but rugged—design and unmatched stability are just two of the reasons, and our Adirondack chair offers all of these benefits, and more.

But unlike most of the Adirondack chair designs available, this one is also very easy to build. There are no complex compound angles to cut, no intricate details on the back and seat slats, and no mortise-and-tenon joints. Like all of the projects in this book, our Adirondack chair can be built by any do-it-yourselfer, using basic tools and simple techniques. And because this design features all the elements of the classic Adirondack chair, your guests and neighbors may never guess that you built it yourself.

We made our Adirondack chair out of cedar and finished it with clear wood sealer. But you may prefer to build your version from pine (a traditional wood for Adirondack furniture), especially if you plan to paint the chair. White, battleship gray and forest green are popular color choices for Adirondack furniture. Be sure to use quality exterior paint with a glossy or enamel finish.

CONSTRUCTION MATERIALS

Quantity	Lumber
1	2 × 6" × 8' cedar
1	2 × 4" × 10' cedar
1	1 × 6" × 14' cedar
1	1 × 4" × 8' cedar
1	1 × 2" × 10' cedar

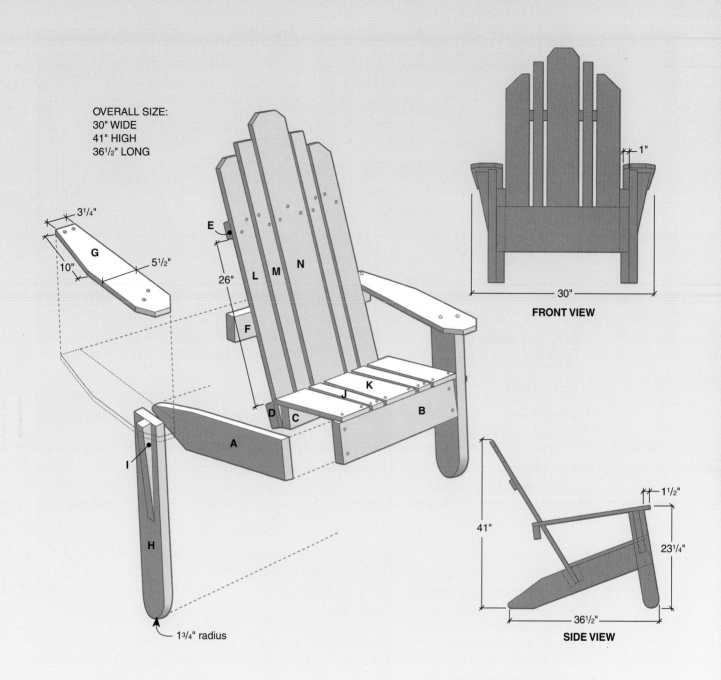

OVERALL SIZE:
30" WIDE
41" HIGH
36½" LONG

FRONT VIEW

SIDE VIEW

1¾" radius

	Cutting List			
Key	**Part**	**Dimension**	**Pcs.**	**Material**
A	Leg	1½ × 5½ × 34½"	2	Cedar
B	Apron	1½ × 5½ × 21"	1	Cedar
C	Seat support	1½ × 3½ × 18"	1	Cedar
D	Low back brace	1½ × 3½ × 18"	1	Cedar
E	High back brace	¾ × 1½ × 18"	1	Cedar
F	Arm cleat	1½ × 3½ × 24"	1	Cedar
G	Arm	¾ × 5½ × 28"	2	Cedar
H	Post	1½ × 3½ × 22"	2	Cedar

	Cutting List			
Key	**Part**	**Dimension**	**Pcs.**	**Material**
I	Arm brace	1½ × 2¼ × 10"	2	Cedar
J	Narrow seat slat	¾ × 1½ × 20¼"	2	Cedar
K	Wide seat slat	¾ × 5½ × 20¼"	3	Cedar
L	End back slat	¾ × 3½ × 36"	2	Cedar
M	Narrow back slat	¾ × 1½ × 38"	2	Cedar
N	Center back slat	¾ × 5½ × 40"	1	Cedar

Materials: Moisture-resistant glue, 1¼", 1½", 2" and 3" deck screws, ⅜ × 2½" lag screws with washers, finishing materials.

Note: Measurements reflect the actual size of dimension lumber.

Cut tapers into the back edges of the legs.

Round the sharp slat edges with a router or a power sander.

Directions:
Adirondack Chair

CUT THE LEGS.
Sprawling back legs that support the seat slats and stretch to the ground on a near-horizontal plane are signature features of the Adirondack style.
1. Cut the legs (A) to length.
2. To make the tapers, mark a point on one end of the board, 2" from the edge. Then, mark another point on the adjacent edge, 6" from the end. Connect the points with a straightedge.
3. Mark a point on the same end, 2¼" in from the other edge. Then, mark a point on that edge, 10" from the end. Connect these points to make a cutting line for the other taper.
4. Cut the two taper cuts with a circular saw.
5. Use the tapered leg as a template to mark and cut identical tapers on the other leg of the chair **(photo A).**

Make decorative cuts on the fronts of the arms (shown) and the tops of the back slats, using a jig saw.

BUILD THE SEAT.
The legs form the sides of the box frame that supports the seat slats. Where counterbores for deck screws are called for, drill holes ¼" deep with a counterbore bit.
1. Cut the apron (B) and seat support (C) to size.
2. Attach the apron to the front ends of the legs with glue and 3" deck screws, in the manner described above.
3. Position the seat support so the inside face is 16½" from the inside edge of the apron. Attach the seat support between the legs, making sure the tops of the parts are flush.
4. Cut the seat slats (J) and (K) to length, and sand the ends smooth. Arrange the slats on

D

Attach the square ends of the posts to the undersides of the arms, being careful to position the part correctly.

top of the seat box, and use wood scraps to set ⅜" spaces between the slats. The slats should overhang the front of the seat box by ¾".

5. Fasten the seat slats by drilling counterbored pilot holes and driving 2" deck screws through the holes and into the tops of the apron and seat support. Keep the counterbores aligned so the cedar plugs form straight lines across the front and back of the seat.

6. Once all the slats are installed, use a router with a ¼" roundover bit (or a power sander) to smooth the edges and ends of the slats **(photo B)**.

MAKE THE BACK SLATS.

The back slats are made from three sizes of dimension lumber.

1. Cut the back slats (L), (M) and (N), to size.

2. Trim the corners on the wider slats. On the 1 × 6 slat (N), mark points 1" in from the outside, top corners. Then, mark points on the outside edges, 1" down from the corners. Connect the

points and trim along the lines with a jig saw. Mark the 1 × 4 slats 2" from one top corner, in both directions. Draw cutting lines and trim.

ATTACH BACK SLATS.

1. Cut the low back brace (D) and high back brace (E) and set them on a flat surface.

2. Slip ¾"-thick spacers under the high brace so the tops of the braces are level. Then, arrange the back slats on top of the braces with ⅝" spacing between slats. The untrimmed ends of the slats should be flush with the bottom edge of the low back brace. The bottom of the high back brace should be 26" above the top of the low brace. The braces must be perpendicular to the slats.

3. Drill pilot holes in the low brace and counterbore the holes. Then, attach the slats to the low brace by driving 2" deck screws through the holes. Follow the same steps for the high brace and attach the slats with 1¼" deck screws.

CUT THE ARMS.

The broad arms of the chair are supported by posts in front, and a cleat attached to the backs of the chair slats.

1. Cut the arms (G) to size.

2. To create decorative angles at the outer end of each arm, mark points 1" from each corner along both edges. Use the points to draw a pair of 1½" cutting lines on each arm. Cut along the lines using a jig saw or circular saw **(photo C)**.

3. As an option, mark points for cutting a tapered cut on the inside, back edge of each arm (see *Diagram*). First, mark points on the back of each arm, 3¼" in from each inside edge. Next, mark the outside edges 10" from the back. Then, connect the points and cut the tapers with a circular saw or jig saw. Sand the edges smooth.

E

F

Drive screws through each post and into an arm brace to stabilize the arm/post joint.

Clamp wood braces to the parts of the chair to hold them in position while you fasten the parts together.

ASSEMBLE THE ARMS, CLEATS AND POSTS.

1. Cut the arm cleat (F) and make a mark 2½" in from each end of the cleat.

2. Set the cleat on edge on your work surface. Position the arms on the top edge of the cleat so the back ends of the arms are flush with the back of the cleat and the untapered edge of each arm is aligned with the 2½" mark. Fasten the arms to the cleats with glue.

3. Drill pilot holes in the arms and counterbore the holes. Drive 3" deck screws through the holes and into the cleat.

4. Cut the posts (H) to size. Then, use a compass to mark a 1¾"-radius roundover cut on each bottom post corner (the roundovers improve stability).

5. Position the arms on top of the square ends of the posts. The posts should be set back 1½" from the front ends of the arm, and 1" from the inside edge of the arm. Fasten the arms to the posts with glue.

6. Drill pilot holes in the arms and counterbore the holes. Then, drive 3" deck screws through the arms and into the posts **(photo D).**

7. Cut tapered arm braces (I) from wood scraps, making sure the grain of the wood runs lengthwise (see page 15). Position an arm brace at the outside of each arm/post joint, centered side to side on the post. Attach each brace with glue.

8. Drill pilot holes in the inside face of the post near the top and counterbore the holes. Then, drive deck screws through the holes and into the brace **(photo E).** Drive a 2" deck screw down through each arm and into the top of the brace.

ASSEMBLE THE CHAIR.

All that remains is to join the back, seat/leg assembly and arm/post assembly to complete construction. Before you start, gather scrap wood to brace the parts while you fasten them.

1. Set the seat/leg assembly on your work surface, clamping a piece of scrap wood to the front apron to raise the front of the assembly until the bottoms of the legs are flush on the surface (about 10").

2. Use a similar technique to

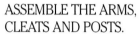

TIP

Making tapered cuts with a circular saw is not difficult if the alignment marks on your saw base are accurate. Before attempting to make a tapered cut where you enter the wood at an angle, always make test cuts on scrap wood to be sure the blade starts cutting in alignment with the alignment marks on your saw. If not, either re-set your alignment marks, or compensate for the difference when you cut the tapers.

brace the arm/post assembly so the bottom of the back cleat is 20" above the work surface. Arrange the assembly so the posts fit around the front of the seat/leg assembly, and the bottom edge of the apron is flush with the front edges of the posts.

3. Drill a ¼"-dia. pilot hole through the inside of each leg and partway into the post. Drive a ⅜ × 2½" lag screw and washer through each hole, but do not tighten completely **(photo F).** Remove the braces.

4. Position the back so the low back brace is between the legs, and the slats are resting against the front of the arm cleat. Clamp the back to the seat support with a C-clamp, making sure the top edge of the low brace is flush with the tops of the legs.

5. Tighten the lag screws at the post/leg joints. Then, add a second lag screw at each joint.

6. Drill three evenly spaced pilot holes near the top edge of the arm cleat and drive 1½" deck screws through the holes and into the back slats **(photo G).** Drive 3" deck screws through the legs and into the ends of the low back brace.

APPLY FINISHING TOUCHES.

1. Glue ¼"-thick, ⅜"-dia. cedar wood plugs into visible counterbores **(photo H).**

2. After the glue dries, sand the plugs even with the surrounding surface. Finish-sand all exposed surfaces with 120-grit sandpaper.

3. Finish the chair as desired— we simply applied a coat of clear wood sealer.

Drive screws through the arm cleat, near the top, and into the slats.

Glue cedar plugs into the counterbores to conceal the screw holes.

Outdoor Storage Center

*Create additional storage space for backyard games and equipment
with this efficient outdoor storage center.*

CONSTRUCTION MATERIALS

Quantity	Lumber
2	⅜" × 4 × 8' textured cedar plywood siding
2	¾" × 2 × 4' BC fir plywood handy panels
2	1 × 2" × 8' cedar
6	1 × 3" × 8' rough-sawn cedar
2	1 × 4" × 8' rough-sawn cedar
1	2 × 2" × 8' pine
1	1 × 2" × 8' pine

Sturdy cedar construction and a rustic appearance make this storage center an excellent addition to any backyard or outdoor setting. The top lid flips up for quick and easy access to the upper shelf storage area, while the bottom doors swing open for access to the lower storage compartments. The raised bottom shelf keeps all stored items up off the ground, where they stay safe and dry. Lawn chairs, yard games, grilling supplies, fishing and boating equipment, and much more can be kept out of sight and protected from the weather. If security is a concern, simply add a locking hasp and padlock to the top lid to keep your property safe and secure. If you have a lot of traffic in and out of the top compartment, add lid support hardware to prop the lid open.

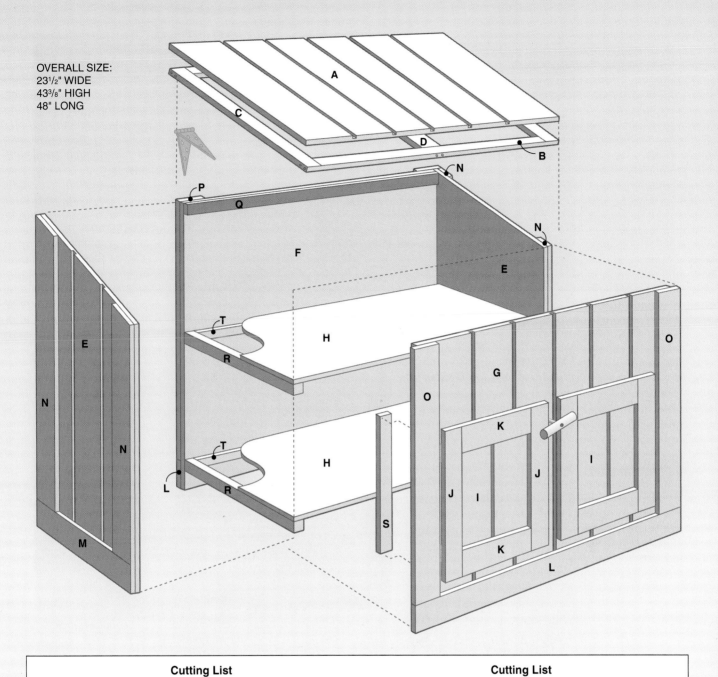

OVERALL SIZE:
23¹/₂" WIDE
43³/₈" HIGH
48" LONG

Key	Part	Dimension	Pcs.	Material
A	Lid	⅝ × 24 × 48"	1	Plywood siding
B	Lid edge	¾ × 1½ × 45"	2	Cedar
C	Lid end	¾ × 1½ × 24"	2	Cedar
D	Lid stringer	¾ × 2½ × 21"	1	Cedar
E	End panel	⅝ × 22 × 42"	2	Plywood siding
F	Back panel	⅝ × 44¾ × 42"	1	Plywood siding
G	Front panel	⅝ × 44¾ × 37½"	1	Plywood siding
H	Shelf	¾ × 20¾ × 44¾"	2	Fir plywood
I	Door panel	⅝ × 15¾ × 17¾"	2	Plywood siding
J	Door stile	¾ × 3½ × 21¼"	4	Cedar
K	Door rail	¾ × 3½ × 12¼"	4	Cedar
L	Kickboard	¾ × 2½ × 47½"	2	Cedar
M	End plate	¾ × 2½ × 22"	2	Cedar
N	End trim	¾ × 2½ × 39½"	4	Cedar
O	Front trim	¾ × 2½ × 35"	2	Cedar
P	Back trim	¾ × 2½ × 39½"	2	Cedar
Q	Hinge cleat	¾ × 1½ × 44¾"	1	Pine
R	Shelf cleat	1½ × 1½ × 20¾"	4	Pine
S	Back cleat	1½ × 1½ × 41¾"	2	Pine
T	Door cleat	¾ × 1½ × 18"	2	Pine

Cutting List (header over both halves of the table)

Materials: Moisture-resistant glue, butt hinges (4), 4" strap hinges (2), 1¼" and 2½" deck screws, door catches (2) or a 1"-dia. × 12" dowel and a ¼"-dia. × 4" carriage bolt, finishing materials.

Note: Measurements reflect actual size of dimension lumber.

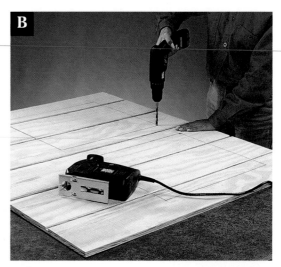

Cut and fasten the lid to the lid framework with the grooves in the panel running back to front.

Drill a ⅜"-dia. starter hole at a corner of each door opening and cut out the openings with a jig saw.

Directions:
Outdoor Storage Center

MAKE THE LID ASSEMBLY.
1. Use a circular saw and a straightedge to cut the lid (A).
2. Cut the lid edges (B), lid ends (C) and lid stringer (D).
3. Lay the lid ends and edges on their faces, smooth side up. Attach the lid ends flush with the outsides of the lid edges, using glue and 2½" deck screws. Attach the lid stringer midway between the lid ends in the same manner.
4. Apply glue to the top faces of the lid ends, stringer and lid edges. Set the lid on the frame assembly **(photo A)** and screw it in place with 1¼" deck screws.

MAKE THE PANELS.
1. Cut the back panel (F) and front panel (G) to size. On the inside face of the front panel, measure up from the bottom and draw straight lines at 5" and 23". Measure in 4" and 20" from each side and draw lines. These lines mark the cutout lines for the door openings.
2. Drill a ⅜"-dia. starter hole at one corner in each door open-

Attach the end panels to the back panel, keeping the back panel flush with the back edges of the end panels.

ing **(photo B).** Cut out the door openings with a jig saw and sand the edges smooth.
3. Cut the end panels (E) to size. On the front edge of each panel, measure down 4½" and place a mark. Draw a line connecting each mark with the top corner on the back edge of the panel, creating cross-cutting lines for the back-to-front tapers. Cross-cut along the lines with a circular saw.

ASSEMBLE THE PANELS.
1. Stand the back panel on its

bottom edge and butt it up between the end panels, flush with the back edges.
2. Fasten the back panel between the side panels with glue and 1¼" deck screws **(photo C).**

ATTACH THE SHELVES.
1. Cut the shelves (H) to size. Measure up 25" from the bottoms of the end panels and draw reference marks for positioning the top shelf. Cut the shelf cleats (R) and back cleats (S) to length. Attach the cleats just below the reference lines

Place the shelf on top of the cleats and fasten with glue and screws.

with glue. Drive 1¼" deck screws through the end panels and back panels and into the cleats.

2. Fasten the shelf to the cleats with 1¼" deck screws **(photo D).** Drive 1¼" deck screws through the back panel and into the shelf.

3. Mark reference lines for the bottom shelf, 4" from the bottoms of the side panels. Install the bottom shelves in the same manner as the top shelves.

4. Fasten the front panel (G) between the end panels with glue and 2½" deck screws.

CUT AND INSTALL TRIM.

1. Cut the kickboards (L), the end plates (M), the end trim (N), the front trim (O) and the back trim (P) to length. Sand the ends smooth. Attach the end plates at the bases of the side panels. Drill ⅛" pilot holes in the end plates. Counterbore the holes ¼" deep, using a counterbore bit. Drive 1¼" deck screws through the end plate and into the side panels.

2. Attach the front and back kickboards to the bases of the front and back panels.

3. Hold the end trim pieces against the side panels at both the front and back edges. Trace the profile of the tapered side panels onto the trim pieces to make cutting lines. The trim pieces at the fronts should be flush with the front panel. Cut at the lines with a circular saw.

4. Attach the end trim pieces to the side panels with 1¼" deck screws **(photo E).** Attach the front and back trim to the front and back panels, covering the edges of the end trim.

ATTACH THE DOORS AND LID.

1. Cut the door stiles (J) and door rails (K) to length. Attach them to the cutout door panels (I), forming a frame that extends 1¾" past the edges of the door panels on all sides.

2. Cut door cleats (T) to length. Screw them to the inside faces of the front panel directly behind the hinge locations at the outside edges of the openings. Mount two butt hinges on the outside edge of each door, using 1¼" deck screws.

3. Install a door catch for each door or use a 1" dowel bolted to the front panel as a turnbuckle.

4. Cut the hinge cleat (Q) to length and attach it to the inside face of the back panel, flush with the top edge.

5. Put the lid and strap hinges in place, with the upper hinge plates positioned between the back trim and lid ends. Drill pilot holes on the back trim for the lower hinge plate and mark the hinge pin location on the back edge of the lid end. Remove the lid and use the location marks to attach the upper hinge plate with 1¼" deck screws. Put the lid in place and attach the lower hinge plates in the same manner.

APPLY FINISHING TOUCHES. Sand edges smooth. Apply a clear wood sealer or any other finish of your choice.

Attach the end trim to the end panel, keeping the front edge of the trim flush with the front edge of the front panel.

Gardener's Tote

*Organize and transport your essential gardening supplies
with this handy cedar tote box.*

CONSTRUCTION MATERIALS

Quantity	Lumber
1	1 × 10" × 6' cedar
1	1 × 6" × 6' cedar
1	1 × 4" × 6' cedar
1	1 × 2" × 6' cedar

This compact carrying tote has plenty of room and is ideal for gardeners. With special compartments sized for seed packages, spray cans and hand tools, it is a quick and easy way to keep your most needed supplies organized and ready to go. The bottom shelf is well suited to storing kneeling pads or towels.

The gentle curves cut into the sides of the storage compartment make for easy access and provide a decorative touch. The sturdy cedar handle has a comfortable hand-grip cutout. You'll find this tote to be an indispensible gardening companion, whether you're tending a small flower patch or a sprawling vegetable garden.

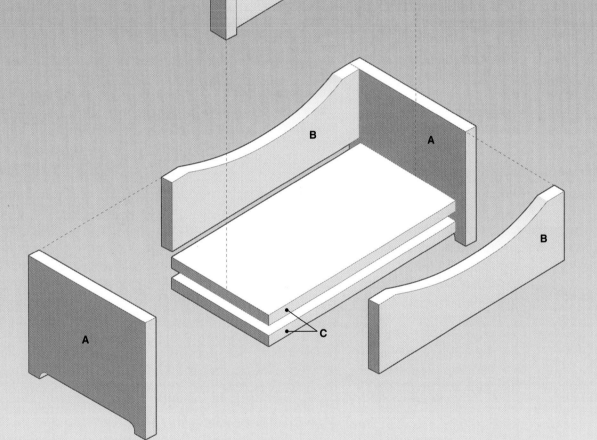

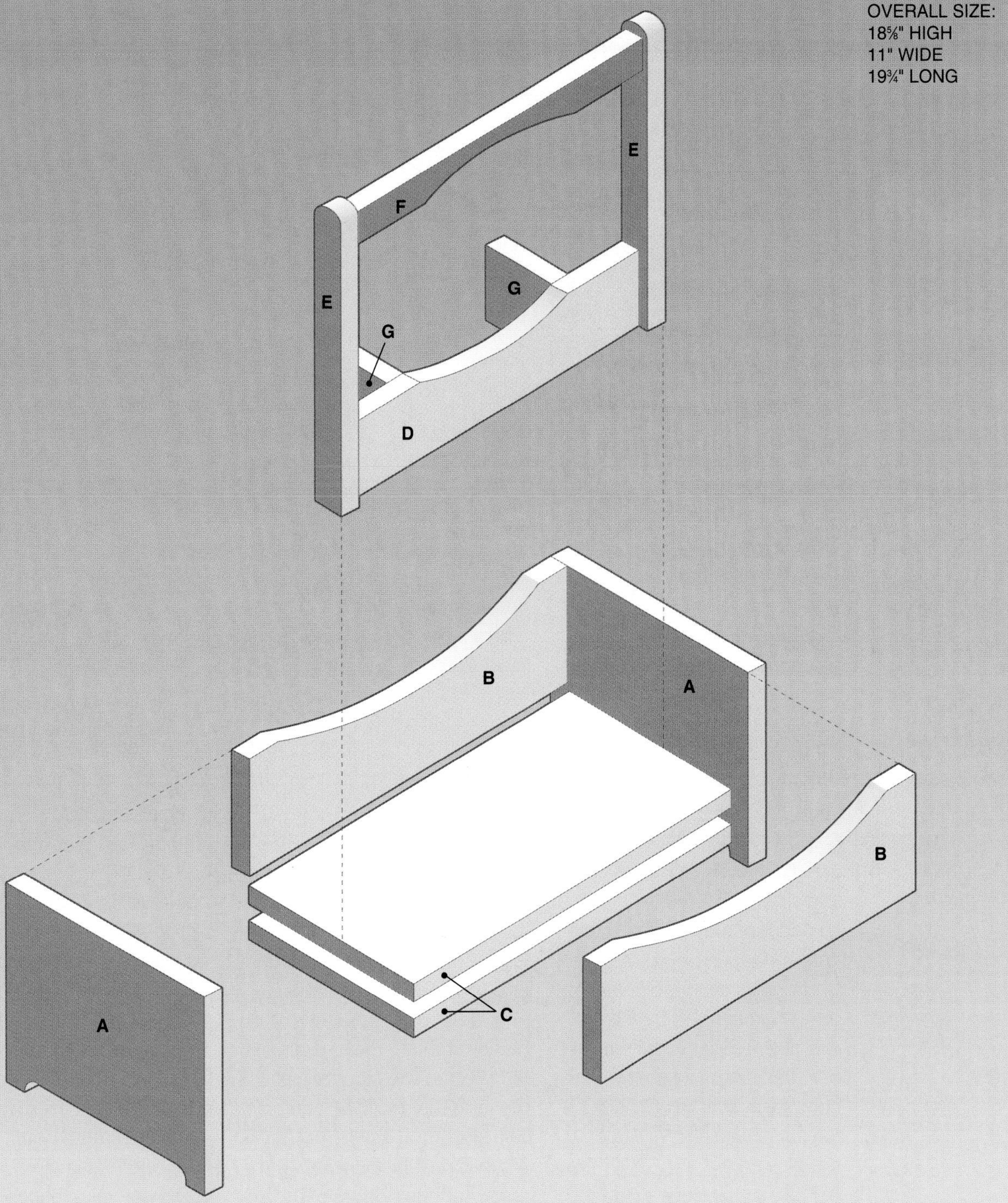

OVERALL SIZE:
18⅝" HIGH
11" WIDE
19¾" LONG

Cutting List				
Key	**Part**	**Dimension**	**Pcs.**	**Material**
A	End	⅞ × 9¼ × 11"	2	Cedar
B	Side	⅞ × 5½ × 18"	2	Cedar
C	Shelf	⅞ × 9¼ × 18"	2	Cedar
D	Divider	⅞ × 3½ × 16¼"	1	Cedar

Cutting List				
Key	**Part**	**Dimension**	**Pcs.**	**Material**
E	Post	⅞ × 1½ × 14"	2	Cedar
F	Handle	⅞ × 1½ × 16¼"	1	Cedar
G	Partition	⅞ × 3½ × 3⅞"	2	Cedar

Materials: Moisture-resistant glue, 1¼" and 2" deck screws, finishing materials.

Note: Measurements reflect the actual size of dimension lumber.

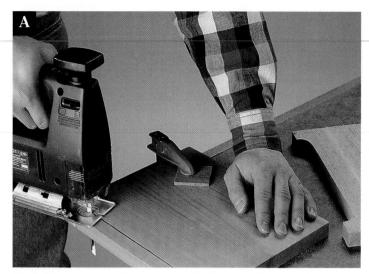

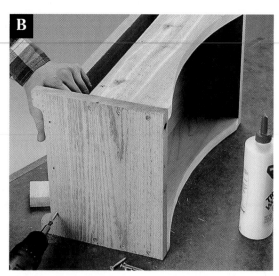

Use a jig saw to cut the curves on the bottom edge of each end, forming feet for the box.

Attach the shelves by driving deck screws through the end pieces and into the ends of the shelves.

Directions: Gardener's Tote

BUILD THE BOX.
The gardener's tote has curved cutouts to improve access and scalloped ends to create feet. All screws are counterbored to ¼" depth for a smooth appearance. A counterbore bit will help you avoid drilling too deep.
1. Cut the ends (A), sides (B) and shelves (C) to size. Sand all parts smooth with medium-grit sandpaper.
2. On one side, mark points on one long edge, 1½" in and 1½" down. Draw a graceful curve between the points to form the cutting line for the curve. Cut the curve with a jig saw and sand it smooth.
3. Position the sides so the edges and ends are flush. Then, trace the curve onto the uncut side and cut it to match. Clamp the sides together, and gang-sand both curves until smooth.
4. Use a compass to draw ¾"-radius semicircles on the bottom edge of the end pieces, with centerpoints 1¾" from each end.
5. Using a straightedge, draw a line connecting the tops of the semicircles to complete the cutout shape. Cut the curves with a jig saw **(photo A),** and sand the ends smooth.
6. To attach the end and side pieces, drill ⅛" pilot holes at each end, 7/16" in from the edges. Position the pilot holes 1", 3" and 5" down from the tops of the ends. Counterbore the holes.
7. Apply glue to the ends of the side pieces—making sure the top and outside edges are flush—and fasten them to the end pieces with 2" deck screws, driven through the end pieces and into the side pieces.
8. Mark the shelf locations on the inside faces of the ends. The bottom of the lower shelf is ¾" up from the bottoms of the ends, and the bottom of the upper shelf is 3¾" up from the bottoms of the ends.
9. Drill pilot holes 7/16" up from the lines. Apply glue to the shelf ends, and position the shelves flush with the lines marked on the end pieces. Drive 2" deck screws through the pilot holes in the end pieces and into the shelves **(photo B).**

BUILD THE DIVIDER ASSEMBLY.
The divider and partitions are assembled first, and then inserted into the box.
1. Cut the divider (D), posts (E), handle (F) and partitions (G) to size.
2. Draw a ⅜"-radius semicircle, using a compass, to mark the cutting line for a roundover at one end of each post. Use a sander to make the roundover.
3. The divider and handle have shallow arcs cut on one long edge. To draw the arcs, mark points 4" in from each end. Then, mark a centered point, ⅝" in from one long edge on the handle. On the divider, mark a centered point, ⅝" in from one long edge.
4. Draw a graceful curve to connect the points, and cut along the lines with a jig saw. Sand the parts smooth.
5. Drill two pilot holes on each end of the divider, 7/16" out from the start of the curve. Counterbore the holes. Attach the divider to the partitions, using glue and 2" deck screws, driven through the divider and

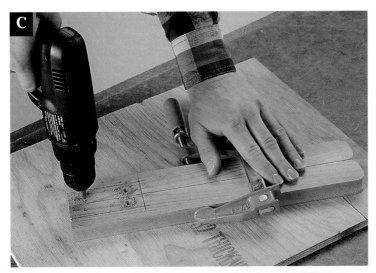

Drill and counterbore pilot holes in the posts before you attach them to the handle and divider.

TIP

Many seed types, soil additives and other common gardening supplies should not be stored outdoors in subfreezing temperatures. If you live in a colder climate, load up your tote with these items in the fall, and store the tote in a warm spot for the winter.

into the edges of the partitions.
6. To mark the positions of the divider ends, clamp the posts together with their edges flush, and mark a 3½"-long reference line on each post, ⅞" from the meeting point between the two posts **(photo C).** Start the reference lines at the square post ends. Connect the lines at the tops to indicate the position of the divider ends.
7. Drill two pilot holes through the posts, centered between each reference line and the inside edge **(photo C).** Counterbore the holes. Drill and counterbore two more pilot holes in each post, centered ½" and 1" down from the tops.
8. Position the handle and divider between the posts, aligned with the pilot holes. One face of the divider should be flush with a post edge. Fasten the handle and divider between the posts with moisture-resistant glue and 2" deck screws, driven through the post holes. Set the assembly in the box. Make sure the partitions fit square with the side.

INSTALL THE DIVIDER ASSEMBLY.
1. Trace position lines for the posts on the end pieces **(photo D).** Apply glue where the posts will be fastened. Drill pilot holes through the posts and counterbore the holes. Then, attach the posts with 1¼" deck screws, driven through the pilot holes and into the ends.
2. Drill two evenly spaced pilot

holes in the side adjacent to the partitions. Counterbore the holes. Then, drive 2" deck screws through the holes and into the edges of the partitions.

APPLY THE FINISHING TOUCHES.
Sand all surfaces smooth with medium (100- or 120-grit) sandpaper. Then finish-sand with fine (150- or 180-grit) sandpaper. If you want to preserve the cedar tones, apply exterior wood stain to all surfaces. Or, you can leave the wood uncoated for a more rustic appearance. As you use the tote, it will slowly turn gray.

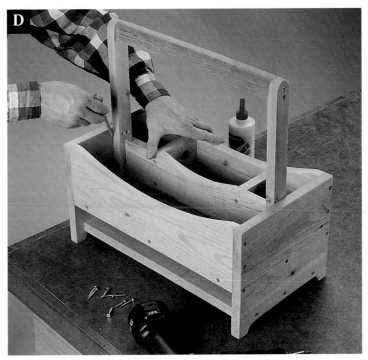

Draw reference lines for the post position on the box ends.

Bird Feeder

*A leftover piece of cedar lap siding is put to good use
in this rustic bird feeder.*

CONSTRUCTION MATERIALS

Quantity	Lumber
1	¾ × 16 × 16" plywood scrap
1	¾" × 6' cedar stop molding
1	8" × 10' cedar lap siding
1	1 × 2" × 8' cedar
1	1"-dia. × 3' dowel

Watching birds feeding in your backyard can be a very relaxing pastime. In this bird feeder project, you will use a piece of 8"-wide cedar lap siding to build a decorative feeder box and then mount it on a piece of scrap plywood. The birds won't mind the leftover building materials. And you'll like the bird feeder because it costs almost nothing to build. Even the plastic viewing window covers that you place inside the feeder box can be made with clear acrylic scrap left over from another project. To fill this cleverly designed bird feeder with seed, turn the threaded rod that serves as a hook so it is aligned with the slot in the roof. Then, simply lift up the roof and add the bird food.

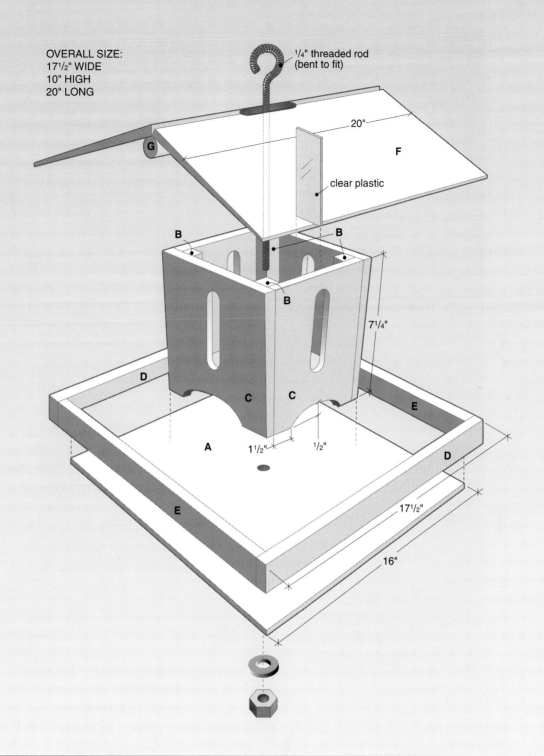

OVERALL SIZE:
17½" WIDE
10" HIGH
20" LONG

¼" threaded rod
(bent to fit)

20"

F

clear plastic

B   B

B

7¼"

D

C   C

E

A

1½"   ½"

E   D

17½"

16"

Cutting List				
Key	**Part**	**Dimension**	**Pcs.**	**Material**
A	Base	¾ × 16 × 16"	1	Plywood
B	Post	¾ × ¾ × 7¼"	4	Cedar
C	Box side	⁵⁄₁₆ × 6 × 7¼"	4	Cedar siding
D	Ledge side	¾ × 1½ × 17½"	2	Cedar

Cutting List				
Key	**Part**	**Dimension**	**Pcs.**	**Material**
E	Ledge end	¾ × 1½ × 16"	2	Cedar
F	Roof panel	⁵⁄₁₆ × 7¼ × 20"	2	Cedar siding
G	Ridge pole	1"-dia. × 20"	1	Dowel

Materials: ¼"-dia. threaded rod with matching nut and washer, hotmelt glue, 4d common nails, rigid acrylic or plastic.

Note: Measurements reflect the actual size of dimension lumber.

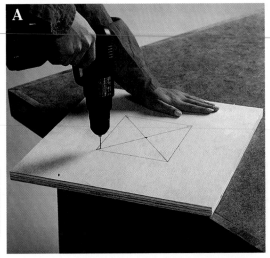

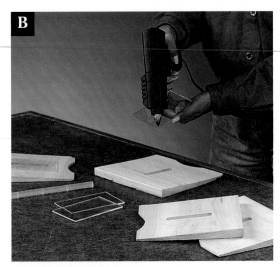

Drill pilot holes in the corners of the feeder box location that is laid out on the plywood base.

Cover the viewing slots by hot-gluing clear plastic or acrylic pieces to the inside face of each panel.

Directions: Bird Feeder

CUT AND PREPARE THE BASE.

The base provides room for several feeding birds and seed.

1. Cut the base (A) from ¾" plywood. Draw straight diagonal lines from corner to corner to locate the center of the base.

2. Measure and mark a 6" square in the middle of the base, making sure the lines are parallel to the edges of the base. This square marks the location for the feeder box.

3. Drill a ¼"-dia. hole through the center of the base where the lines cross.

4. Measure in toward the center ⅜" from each corner of the 6" square and mark points. Drill ¹⁄₁₆" pilot holes all the way through at these points **(photo A).**

PREPARE THE FEEDER BOX PARTS.

The posts and box sides form the walls of the feeder box. Vertical grooves in the box

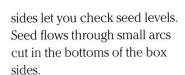

Mark the profile of the bevel of the siding onto two of the box sides for trimming.

sides let you check seed levels. Seed flows through small arcs cut in the bottoms of the box sides.

1. Cut the posts (B) to length from ¾"-square cedar stop molding. (Or, rip a 3'-long piece of ¾"-thick cedar to ¾" in width to make the posts.)

2. From 8" cedar lap siding (actual dimension is 7¼") cut two 6"-wide box sides (C). Then, cut two more panels to about 7" in width to be trimmed later to follow the lap-siding bevels.

3. Cut viewing slots. First, drill two ½" starter holes for a jig saw blade along the center of each box side—one hole 2" from the

top, and the other 2" from the bottom. Connect the starter holes by cutting with a jig saw to form the slots.

4. Cut a ½"-deep arc into the bottom of each box side, using the jig saw. Start the cuts 1½" from each end. Smooth out the arcs with a drum sander on a power drill.

5. Cut strips of clear acrylic or plastic slightly larger than the viewing slots. Hot-glue them over the slots on the inside of the box sides **(photo B).**

6. To mark cutting lines for trimming two of the box sides to follow the siding bevel, tape the box sides together into a

TIPS

Hotmelt glue is often thought of as primarily a product for craftmaking and indoor patch-up jobs. But for lightweight exterior projects, it is a very effective adhesive. The hot glue penetrates deeply into the pores of cedar, and creates a strong, durable bond between wood parts.

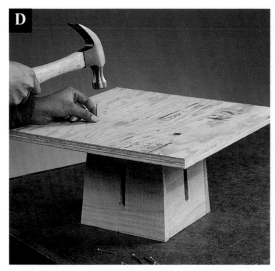

Drive 4d common nails through pilot holes to fasten the feeder box to the base.

Insert spacers 2" in from the "eaves" of the roof to set the pitch before applying glue to the seam.

box shape. The wide ends of the beveled siding should all be flush. Trace the siding profile onto the inside faces of the two box ends **(photo C).** Disassemble the box. Cut along the profile lines with a jig saw.

ASSEMBLE THE FEEDER BOX.
1. Hot-glue the posts flush with the inside edges on the box sides that were trimmed in Step 6 (above).
2. Hot-glue the untrimmed box sides to the posts.

ATTACH THE BASE.
1. Align the assembled feeder box with the 6" square outline on the base. Hot-glue the box to the base on these lines. Turn the assembly upside down.
2. Attach the base to the feeder box by driving 4d galvanized common nails through the pre-drilled pilot holes in the base, and into the posts on the feeder box **(photo D).**
3. Cut the ledge sides (D) and ledge ends (E) to length. Next, build a frame around the base that prevents seed spills. Using hot glue, attach the ledge

pieces so the bottoms are flush with the bottom of the base. Reinforce the joint with 4d common nails.

MAKE THE ROOF.
1. Cut the ridge pole (G) from a 1"-dia. dowel. Cut the roof panels (F) from 8" siding.
2. To create the roof pitch, lay the panels on your work surface so the wide ends butt together. Place a 1"-thick spacer under each of the narrow ends, 2" in from each end.
3. Apply a heavy bead of hot glue into the seam between the panels **(photo E).** Quickly press the ridge pole into the seam. Let the glue harden for at least 15 minutes.
4. Set the roof right-side-up, and rest each end of the ridge pole on a 2 × 4 block. Drill ⅜" starter holes down through the roof and the ridge pole, 1" to either side of the ridge's midpoint. Connect the starter holes by cutting a slot between them, using a jig saw. Widen the slot until the ¼"-dia. threaded rod passes through with minimal resistance.
5. Cut the threaded rod to 16"

in length. Use pliers to bend a 1½"-dia. loop in one end of the rod. Place the roof on the feeder box. Then, thread the unbent end of the rod through the roof and the hole in the base **(photo F).** Spin the rod loop so it is perpendicular to the roof ridge.
6. Tighten a washer and nut onto the end of the rod, loosely enough so the loop can be spun with moderate effort. For a rustic look, don't apply a finish to your bird feeder.

The bird feeder is held together by a looped, threaded rod that runs through the roof and is secured with a washer and nut on the underside of the base.

Bird Feeder Stand

Send an invitation to flocks of colorful backyard guests by hanging bird feeders from this sturdy cedar stand.

Create a hub of avian activity in your backyard by building this clever bird feeder stand. Bird feeders vary widely in size and style—from small and plain to large and fanciful. This stand can support more than one kind of bird feeder at a time, letting you show off your favorite types. If you want to attract different species of birds to your feeding area, hang feeders that contain different foods. Then sit and enjoy the sight of a variety of birds fluttering and roosting in one central area.

One important benefit of this cedar bird feeder stand is that it has a freestanding, open de-sign. Birds are always in full view as they eat.

The heavy stand base, made from cedar frames, provides ample support for the post and hanging arms. To simplify cleanup of any spilled food (and to make it accessible to hungry birds), you can attach a layer of window screening over the slats in the top of the base. Cleaning the bird feeder stand is easy—just remove the feeders, tip the stand on its side and spray it down with a hose.

CONSTRUCTION MATERIALS

Quantity	Lumber
1	1 × 4" × 8' cedar
1	1 × 4" × 10' cedar
2	1 × 4" × 12' cedar
2	1 × 6" × 12' cedar
2	2 × 4" × 12' cedar
1	2 × 6" × 6' cedar

OVERALL SIZE:
72" HIGH
35¼" WIDE
35¼" LONG

1" squares

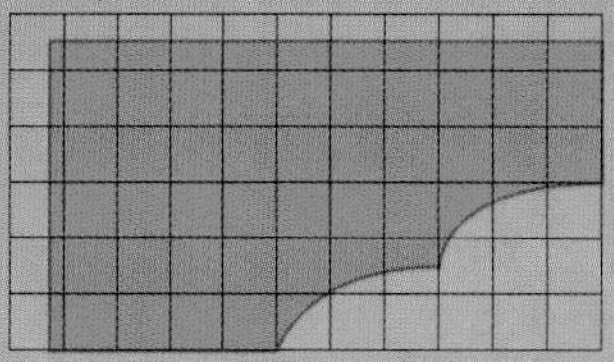

PART H DETAIL

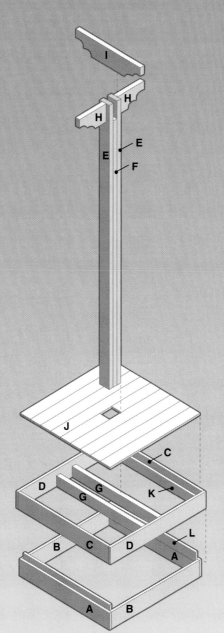

		Cutting List					Cutting List		
Key	**Part**	**Dimension**	**Pcs.**	**Material**	**Key**	**Part**	**Dimension**	**Pcs.**	**Material**
A	Bottom end	⅞ × 5½ × 33½"	2	Cedar	**G**	Post support	1½ × 3½ × 33½"	2	Cedar
B	Bottom side	⅞ × 5½ × 31¾"	2	Cedar	**H**	Outside arm	1½ × 5½ × 10¼"	2	Cedar
C	Top end	⅞ × 5½ × 33½"	2	Cedar	**I**	Inside arm	1½ × 5½ × 36"	1	Cedar
D	Top side	⅞ × 5½ × 35¼"	2	Cedar	**J**	Floor board	⅞ × 3½ × 33½"	9	Cedar
E	Post board	1½ × 3½ × 72"	2	Cedar	**K**	Floor support	⅞ × 3½ × 33½"	2	Cedar
F	Center board	1½ × 3½ × 66½"	1	Cedar	**L**	Bottom cleat	⅞ × 3½ × 31¾"	2	Cedar

Materials: 1½" and 2½" deck screws, 18 × 36" window screening (2), eye hooks, finishing materials.

Note: Measurements reflect the actual size of dimension lumber.

Join the top base frame to the bottom base frame by driving screws through the frame cleats.

Use a square to make sure the inside arm is perpendicular to the post before you secure it into the gap at the top of the post.

Directions:
Bird Feeder Stand

BUILD THE BASE FRAMES.
1. Cut the bottom ends (A), bottom sides (B), top ends (C) and top sides (D) to length. Sand the parts smooth. Drill ⅛" pilot holes near the ends of the bottom ends and counterbore the holes to a ¼" depth with a counterbore bit. Fasten the bottom sides between the bottom ends by driving 1½" deck screws through the pilot holes. Repeat this procedure with the top sides and top ends to complete the second base frame.
2. Cut the floor supports (K) to length. Fasten them to the inside faces of the top ends so the bottoms of the supports are flush with the bottoms of the ends. Cut the bottom cleats (L) to length. Attach them

with 1½" deck screws to the inside faces of the bottom ends. Make sure the top edge of each bottom cleat is 1½" above the top edge of each bottom end.
3. Set the top frame over the bottom frame. Fasten the top and bottom frames together by driving deck screws through the bottom cleats and into the top frame **(photo A).**

INSTALL POST SUPPORTS.
1. Mark the centerpoints of the top sides on their inside faces. Draw reference lines, 2¼" to each side of the centerpoints. These lines mark the locations for the post supports (G).
2. Cut the post supports to length. Place them in the top frame so their bottom edges rest on the tops of the bottom sides. Position the post supports with their inside faces just outside the reference lines. Drill pilot holes through the frame and counterbore the holes. Fasten the post supports to the top frame by driving 2½" deck screws through the frame and into the supports.

BUILD THE ARMS.
1. Cut the two outside arms (H) and the inside arm (I) to length. Use a pencil to draw a 1"-square grid pattern on one of the arms. Using the grid patterns as a reference (see *Diagram,* page 33), lay out the decorative scallops at the end of the arm.
2. Cut along the layout lines with a jig saw. With a 1"-dia. drum sander mounted in an electric drill, smooth the insides of the curves. Use the arm as a template to draw identical scallops on the other arms. Then, cut and sand the other arms to match.

MAKE THE POST.
The post is constructed by sandwiching the center board (F) between two post boards (E). It's easiest to attach the outside arms before you assemble the post.
1. Cut the post boards (E) to length and draw 5½"-long center lines on one face of each post board, starting at the top. Then, draw a 5½"-long line, ¾"

to each side of the center line, to mark the outlines for the outside arms on the post. On the center line, drill pilot holes for the deck screws, 1½" and 4½" down from the top edge. Counterbore the holes.

2. Attach the outside arms to the side posts by driving 2½" deck screws through the posts and into the straight ends of the outside arms. Sandwich the center board between the side post boards, with the bottom and side edges flush.

3. Drive pairs of 2½" deck screws at 8" to 12" intervals, screwing through the face of one post board. Then, flip the assembly over and drive screws through the other post board. Make sure to stagger them so you don't hit screws driven from the other side.

4. Center the inside arm in the gap at the top of the post **(photo B).** Then, drive 2½" deck screws through the post boards and into the inside arm.

5. Install the post assembly by standing the post up between the post supports in the base frame. Be sure the post is centered between the top frame sides and is perpendicular to the post supports. Drive 2½" deck screws through the post supports and into the post to secure the parts.

MAKE THE FEEDING FLOOR.

Floor boards are attached to the floor supports within the top base frame.

1. Cut the floor boards (J) to length. One floor board should be cut into two 14½"-long pieces to fit between the post and frame.

2. Arrange the floor boards across the post supports and

Attach the floor boards by driving deck screws through the floor boards and into the post and floor supports.

floor supports, using ¼"-wide scraps to set ¼"-wide gaps between the boards.

3. To fasten the floor boards to the floor supports and post supports, first drill pilot holes in the floor boards and counterbore the holes. Then, drive 1½" deck screws through the pilot holes and into the floor supports **(photo C).**

APPLY FINISHING TOUCHES.

1. Apply exterior wood stain to the bird feeder stand. After it dries, staple two 18 × 36" strips of window screening to the floor to keep food from falling through the gaps **(photo D).**

2. Insert brass screw eyes or other hardware at the ends of the arms to hang your bird feeders. Set the stand in a semi-sheltered area in clear view of your favorite window or deck.

Staple window screening over the tops of the floor boards to keep bird food from falling through the gaps.

Freestanding Arbor

Create a shady retreat on a sunny patio or deck with this striking arbor.

This freestanding arbor combines the beauty and durability of natural cedar with an Oriental-inspired design. Set it up on your patio or deck, or in a quiet corner of your backyard—it adds just the right finishing touch to turn your outdoor living space into a showplace geared for relaxation and quiet contemplation. The arbor has a long history as a focal point in gardens and other outdoor areas throughout the world. And if privacy and

shade are concerns, you can enhance the sheltering quality by adding climbing vines that weave their way in and out of the trellis. Or simply set a few potted plants around the base to help the arbor blend in with the outdoor environment. Another way to integrate plant life into your arbor is to hang decorative potted plants from the top beams.

This arbor is freestanding, so it easily can be moved to a new

site whenever you desire. Or, you can anchor it permanently to a deck or to the ground and equip it with a built-in seat.

Sturdy posts made from 2 × 4 cedar serve as the base of the arbor, forming a framework for a 1 × 2 trellis system that scales the sides and top. The curved cutouts that give the arbor its Oriental appeal are made with a jig saw, then smoothed out with a drill and drum sander for a more finished appearance.

CONSTRUCTION MATERIALS

Quantity	Lumber
2	1 × 2" × 8' cedar
5	2 × 2" × 8' cedar
9	2 × 4" × 8' cedar
3	2 × 6" × 8' cedar

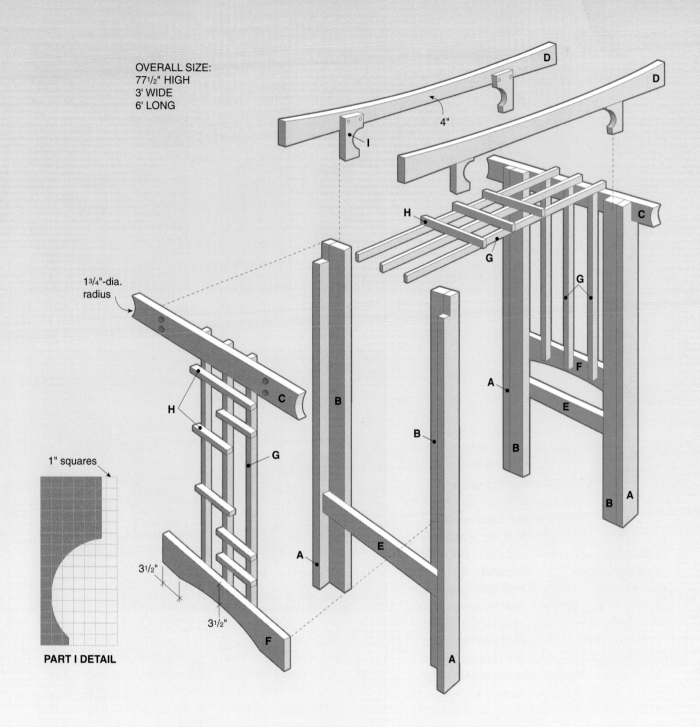

OVERALL SIZE:
77½" HIGH
3' WIDE
6' LONG

4"

I

D

D

C

H

G

G

G

1¾"-dia. radius

H

C

G

B

A

B

F

E

A

B

E

A

B

B

A

1" squares

PART I DETAIL

3½"

3½"

F

A

Cutting List				
Key	Part	Dimension	Pcs.	Material
A	Leg front	1½ × 3½ × 72"	4	Cedar
B	Leg side	1½ × 3½ × 72"	4	Cedar
C	Cross beam	1½ × 3½ × 36"	2	Cedar
D	Top beam	1½ × 5½ × 72"	2	Cedar
E	Side rail	1½ × 3½ × 21"	2	Cedar

Cutting List				
Key	Part	Dimension	Pcs.	Material
F	Side spreader	1½ × 5½ × 21"	2	Cedar
G	Trellis strip	⅞ × 1½ × 48"	9	Cedar
H	Cross strip	⅞ × 1½ × *	15	Cedar
I	Brace	1½ × 5½ × 15"	4	Cedar

Materials: Wood glue, wood sealer or stain, #10 × 2½" wood screws, ⅜"-dia. × 2½" lag screws (8), 6" lag screws (4), 2½" and 3" deck screws, finishing materials.

Note: Measurements reflect the actual size of dimension lumber.

*Cut to fit

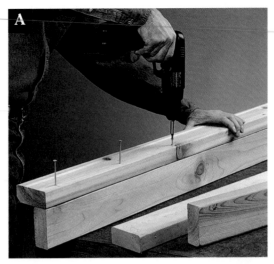

Create four legs by fastening leg sides to leg fronts at right angles.

Cut a notch in the top of each of the four legs to hold the cross beams.

Directions:
Freestanding Arbor

MAKE THE LEGS.

Each of the four arbor legs is made from two 6'-long pieces of 2 × 4 cedar, fastened at right angles with 3" deck screws.

1. Cut the leg fronts (A) and leg sides (B) to length. Position the leg sides at right angles to the leg fronts, with top and bottom edges flush. Apply moisture-resistant glue to the joint. Attach the leg fronts to the leg sides by driving evenly spaced screws through the faces of the fronts and into the edges of the sides **(photo A).**

2. Use a jig saw to cut a 3½"-long × 2"-wide notch at the top outside corner of each leg front **(photo B).** These notches cradle the cross beams when the arbor is assembled.

MAKE THE CROSS BEAMS, RAILS & SPREADERS.

1. Cut cross beams (C) to

A piece of cardboard acts as a template when you trace the outline for the arc on the cross beams.

length. Cut a small arc at both ends of each cross beam. Start by using a compass to draw a 3½"-diameter semicircle at the edge of a strip of cardboard. Cut out the semicircle, and use the strip as a template for marking the arcs **(photo C).** Cut out the arcs with a jig saw. Sand the cuts smooth with a drill and drum sander.

2. Cut two spreaders (F) to length. The spreaders fit just above the rails on each side. Mark a curved cutting line on the bottom of each spreader

(see *Diagram*, page 37). To mark the cutting lines, draw starting points 3½" in from each end of a spreader. Make a reference line 2" up from the bottom of the spreader board. Tack a casing nail on the reference line, centered between the ends of the spreader. With the spreader clamped to the work surface, also tack nails into the work surface next to the starting lines on the spreader. Slip a thin strip of metal or plastic between the casing nails so the strip bows

Lag-screw the cross beams to the legs, and fasten the spreaders and rails with deck screws to assemble the side frames.

Attach trellis strips to the cross brace and spreader with deck screws.

Also set a spreader and a rail between the legs for spacing.
2. Drill ⅜" pilot holes in the cross beam. Counterbore the holes to a ¼" depth, using a counterbore bit. Attach the cross beam to each leg with glue. Drive two ⅜"-dia. × 2½" lag screws through the cross beam and into the legs **(photo D).**
3. Position the spreader between the legs so the top is 29½" up from the bottoms of the legs. Position the rail 18" up from the leg bottoms. Drill ⅛" pilot holes in the spreader and rail. Counterbore the holes. Keeping the legs parallel, attach the pieces with glue and drive 3" deck screws through the outside faces of the legs and into the rail and spreader.

ATTACH THE SIDE TRELLIS PIECES.

Each side trellis is made from vertical strips of cedar 2 × 2 that are fastened to the side frames. Horizontal cross strips will be added later to create a decorative cross-hatching effect.
1. Cut three vertical trellis strips (G) to length for each side frame. Space them so they are 2⅜" apart, with the ends flush with the top of the cross beam **(photo E).**
2. Drill pilot holes to attach the trellis strips to the cross beam and spreader. Counterbore the holes and drive 2½" deck screws. Repeat the procedure for the other side frame.

out to create a smooth arc. Trace the arc onto the spreader, then cut along the line with a jig saw. Smooth with a drum sander. Use the first spreader as a template for marking and cutting the second spreader.
3. Cut the rails (E) to length. They are fitted between pairs of legs on each side of the arbor, near the bottom, to keep the arbor square.

ASSEMBLE THE SIDE FRAMES.

Each side frame consists of a front and back leg, joined together by a rail, spreader and cross beam.
1. Lay two leg assemblies parallel on a work surface, with the notched board in each leg facing up. Space the legs so the inside faces of the notched boards are 21" apart. Set a cross beam into the notches, overhanging each leg by 6".

Use long pieces of 1 × 4 to brace the side frames in an upright, level position while you attach the top beams.

Lock the legs in a square position after assembling the arbor by tacking strips of wood between the front legs and between the back legs.

CUT AND SHAPE TOP BEAMS.

1. Cut two top beams (D) to length. Draw 1½"-deep arcs at the top edges of the top beams, starting at the ends of each of the boards.

2. Cut the arcs into the top beams with a jig saw. Sand smooth with a drum sander.

TIP

There are no firm rules about arbor placement. It can be positioned to provide a focal point for a porch, patio or deck. Placed against a wall or at the end of a plain surface, arbors improve the general look of the area. With some thick, climbing vines and vegetation added to the arbor, you can also disguise a utility area, such as a trash collection space.

ASSEMBLE TOP AND SIDES.

1. Because the side frames are fairly heavy and bulky, you will need to brace them in an upright position to fasten the top beams between them. A simple way to do this is to use a pair of 1 × 4 braces to connect the tops and bottoms of the side frames **(photo F)**. Clamp the ends of the braces to the side frames so the side frames are 4' apart, and use a level to make sure the side frames are plumb.

2. Mark a centerpoint for a lag bolt 12¾" from each end of each top beam. Drill a ¼" pilot hole through the top edge at the centerpoint. Set the top beams on top of the cross braces of the side frames. Mark the pilot hole locations onto

the cross beams. Remove the top beams and drill pilot holes into the cross beams. Secure the top beams to the cross beams with 6" lag screws.

3. Cut four braces (I) to length, and transfer the brace cutout pattern from the *Diagram* on page 37 to each board. Cut the patterns with a jig saw. Attach the braces at the joints where the leg fronts meet the top beams, using 2½" deck screws. To make sure the arbor assembly stays in position while you complete the project, attach 1 × 2 scraps between the front legs and between the back legs **(photo G)**.

4. Cut and attach three trellis strips (G) between the top beams.

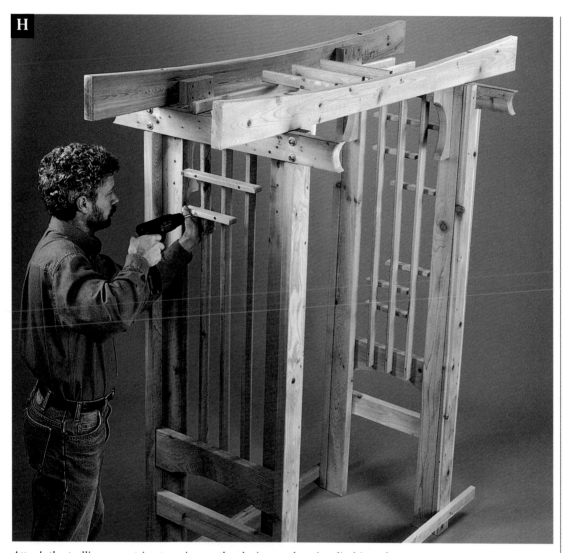

Attach the trellis cross strips to spice up the design and assist climbing plants.

ADD TRELLIS CROSS STRIPS.

1. Cut the cross strips (H) to 7" and 10" lengths. Use wood screws to attach them at 3" intervals in a staggered pattern on the side trellis pieces **(photo H).** You can adjust the sizes and placement of the cross strips but, for best appearance, retain some symmetry of placement.

2. Fasten cross strips to the top trellis in the same manner. Make sure the cross strips that fit across the top trellis are arranged in similar fashion to the side strips.

APPLY FINISHING TOUCHES.

1. To protect the arbor, coat the cedar wood with clear wood sealer. After the finish dries, the arbor is ready to be placed onto your deck or patio or in a quiet corner of your yard.

2. Because of its sturdy construction, the arbor can simply be set onto a hard, flat surface. If you plan to install a permanent seat in the arbor, you should anchor it to the ground. For decks, try to position the arbor so you can screw the legs to the rim of the deck or toenail the legs into the deck boards. You can buy fabricated metal post stakes, available at most building centers, to use when anchoring the arbor to the ground.

> TIP
>
> *Create an arbor seat by resting two 2 × 10 cedar boards on the rails in each side frame. Overhang the rails by 6" or so, and drive a few 3" deck screws through the boards and into the rails to secure the seat.*

Yard & Garden Cart

With a 4-cubic-foot bin and a built-in rack for long-handled tools, this sleek utility cart is hardworking and versatile.

CONSTRUCTION MATERIALS	
Quantity	**Lumber**
1	2 × 6" × 8' cedar
4	2 × 4" × 8' cedar
2	1 × 6" × 8' cedar
2	1 × 4" × 8' cedar
1	1"-dia. × 3' dowel

This sturdy yard-and-garden cart picks up where a plain wheelbarrow leaves off. It includes many clever features that help make doing yard work more efficient, without sacrificing hauling capacity. And because it's made of wood, this cart will never dent or rust.

The notches in the handle frame keep long-handled tools from being jostled about as the cart rolls across your yard. The handle itself folds down and locks in place like a kick-stand when the cart is parked. When you're pushing the cart, the handle flips up to form an extra-long handle that takes advantage of simple physics to make the cart easier to push and steer.

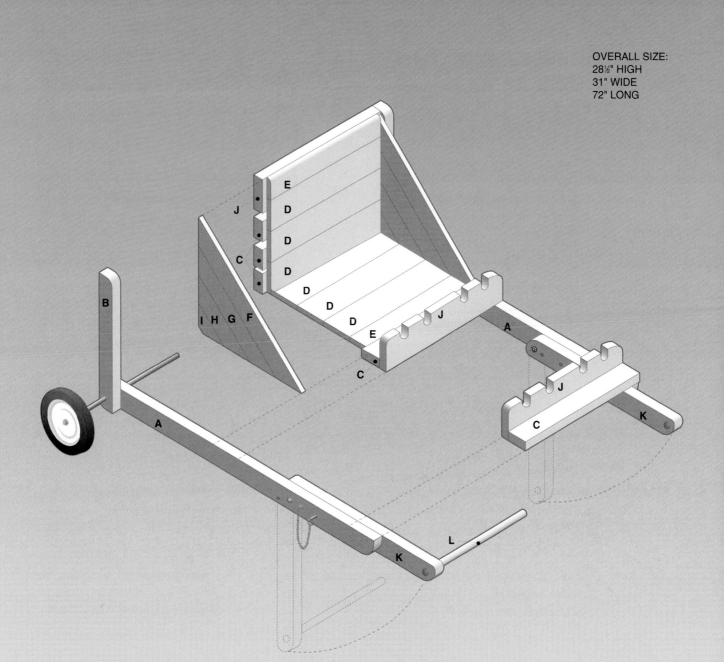

OVERALL SIZE:
28½" HIGH
31" WIDE
72" LONG

Cutting List

Key	Part	Dimension	Pcs.	Material
A	Back support	1½ × 3½ × 57"	2	Cedar
B	Front support	1½ × 3½ × 23½"	2	Cedar
C	Cross rail	1½ × 3½ × 24"	5	Cedar
D	Bin slat	⅞ × 5½ × 22¼"	6	Cedar
E	End slat	⅞ × 3½ × 22¼"	2	Cedar
F	Bin side	⅞ × 3½ × 28"	2	Cedar

Cutting List

Key	Part	Dimension	Pcs.	Material
G	Bin side	⅞ × 3½ × 21"	2	Cedar
H	Bin side	⅞ × 3½ × 14"	2	Cedar
I	Bin side	⅞ × 3½ × 7"	2	Cedar
J	Top rail	1½ × 5½ × 24"	3	Cedar
K	Arm	1½ × 3½ × 32"	2	Cedar
L	Handle	1"-dia. × 20⅞"	1	Dowel

Materials: 2" and 2½" deck screws, 4d finish nails (2), 10" utility wheels (2), 30" steel axle rod, ³⁄₁₆"-dia. cotter pins, ⅜"-dia. hitch pins and chain (2), ⅜ × 4" carriage bolts (2) with lock nuts (2) and washers (4), finishing materials.

Note: Measurements reflect the actual size of dimension lumber.

Test with a square to make sure the front supports and back supports are joined at right angles.

Make straight cuts from the edge of each rail to the sides of the holes to make the tool notches.

Directions:
Yard & Garden Cart

BUILD THE CART FRAME.
Counterbore all pilot holes in this project, using a counterbore bit, so the screw heads are recessed for improved safety and visual appeal.

1. Cut the back supports (A), front supports (B), three cross rails (C) and one of the top rails (J) to length.

2. Use a compass to draw a curve with a 3½" radius on each end of the back supports on the same side, and on each end of the front supports on opposite sides. When the curves are cut, the ends of these parts will have one rounded corner and one square corner. Cut the curves with a jig saw and sand out any rough spots or saw marks.

3. Position a top rail between the ends of the front supports, flush with the square corners of the front supports. Drill ⅛" pilot holes in the supports. Counterbore the holes ¼" deep, using a counterbore bit. Fasten the rail between the supports with glue and drive 2½" deck screws through the supports and into the rail.

4. Position two cross rails between the front supports, 7½" and 13" down from the top ends of the front supports. Make sure the cross rails are aligned with the top rail. Attach them with glue and 2½" deck screws. Fasten another cross rail between the bottom ends of the front supports. The bottom edge of this cross rail should be 3½" up from the bottoms of the front supports and aligned with the other rails.

5. Attach the front supports to the back supports with glue and 2½" deck screws, using a square to make sure the parts are joined at right angles

(photo A). The unshaped ends of the back supports should be flush with the front and bottom edges of the front supports, and the back supports should be attached to the inside faces of the front supports.

6. Drill centered, ½"-dia. holes for the wheel axles through the bottoms of the front supports and back supports. Position the holes 1¾" from both the bottom ends and the sides of the front supports.

CUT THE NOTCHED
TOP RAILS.

1. Cut the two remaining top rails (J) to length. These rails contain notches that are aligned to create a tool rack. Before cutting the notches, use a compass to draw 1½"-radius roundover curves at each end along one side of each rail. Cut the roundovers with a jig saw.

2. To make the tool notches in the top rails, first draw a reference line 1½" in from the rail edge between the roundovers. Mark four drilling points on the line, 3¾" and 8¼" in from each

TIP

If you need to round over the end of a board, one easy solution that gets good results is to use your belt sander like a bench grinder. Simply mount the belt sander to a work surface sideways, so the belt is perpendicular to the work surface and has room to spin. Turn on the sander, lay your workpiece on the work surface, and grind away.

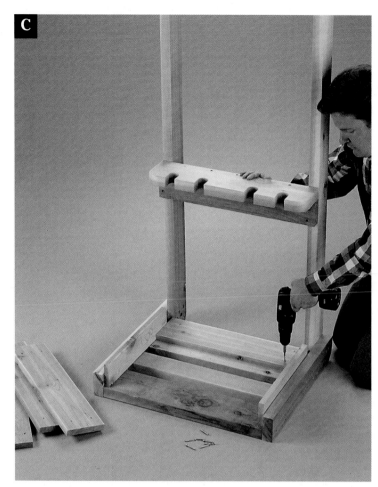

Attach the bin slats to the front supports, leaving a ⅞"-wide gap at both ends of each slat.

end. Use a drill and a spade bit to drill 1½"-dia. holes through the drilling points on each rail.
3. Use a square to draw cutting lines from the sides of the holes to the near edge of each rail. Cut along the lines with a jig saw to complete the tool notches **(photo B).**

ATTACH RAILS BETWEEN THE BACK SUPPORTS.

1. Cut two cross rails (C) to length and lay them flat on your work surface. Attach a top rail to one edge of each cross rail, so the ends are flush and the notched edges of the top rails are facing up. Drive 2½" deck screws at 4" intervals through the top rails and into the edges of the cross rails.

2. Set one of the assemblies on the free ends of the back supports, flush with the edges. The free edge of the cross rail should be flush with the ends of the back supports. Attach the cross rail with 2½"deck screws driven down into the back support.

3. Attach the other rail assembly to the top edges of the back supports so the top rail faces the other rail assembly, and the free edge of the cross rail is 22⅜" from the front ends of the back supports.

ATTACH THE BIN SLATS.

1. Cut the bin slats (D) and end slats (E) to length. Position one end slat and three bin slats be-

tween the front supports, with the edge of the end slat flush with the edge of the top rail and the last bin slat butted against the back supports. There should be a ⅞" gap between the ends of each slat and the front supports. Attach the slats with glue and 2" deck screws driven down through the slats and into the cross rails and top rail **(photo C).**

2. Fasten the rest of the bin slats to the top edges of the back supports, with a ⅞" recess at each end. Start at the bottom of the bin, and work your way up, driving 2½" deck screws through the slats and into the tops of the back supports. Fasten the end slat between the last bin slat and the lower cross rail on the back supports.

3. Use a grinder or belt sander with a coarse belt to round the front edges of the front end slat **(photo D).**

ATTACH THE BIN SIDES.

1. Square-cut the bin sides (F, G, H, I) to the lengths shown in the *Cutting List,* page 43. Draw a 45° miter-cutting line at each end of each bin side. Make the miter cuts with a circular saw and straightedge, or with a power miter saw.

2. Fit the short, V-shaped sides into the recesses at the sides of the bin, and attach them to the front supports with glue and 2"

TIP

Cut pieces of sheet aluminum or galvanized metal to line the cart bin for easy cleaning after hauling. Simply cut the pieces to fit inside the bin, then attach them with special roofing nails that have rubber gaskets under the nail heads. Make sure that no sharp metal edges are sticking out from the bin.

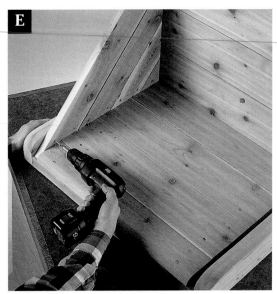

Round the tips of the front supports and the front edge of the end slat, using a belt sander.

Fasten the bin sides in a V-shape with glue and deck screws.

Drill a pilot hole through each arm and into the ends of the handle, then drive 4d finish nails into the holes to secure the handle.

ATTACH THE ARMS.

1. Drill ⅜"-dia. holes for carriage bolts through each back support, 19" from the handle end, and centered between the top and bottom edges of the supports.

2. Insert a ⅜"-dia. × 4"-long carriage bolt through the outside of each ⅜"-dia. hole in the back supports. Slip a washer over each bolt, then slip the arms over the carriage bolts. Slip another washer over the end of each bolt, then secure the arms to the supports by tightening a lock nut onto each bolt. Do not overtighten the lock nut—the arms need to be loose enough to pivot freely.

3. Cut the handle (L) to length from a 1"-dia. dowel (preferably hardwood). Slide it into the 1"-dia. holes in the ends of the arms. Secure the handle by drilling pilot holes for 4d finish nails through each arm and into the dowel **(photo F).** Then, drive a finish nail into the dowel at each end.

deck screws. Install the rest of the bin sides **(photo E).**

MAKE THE ARMS.

The arms serve a dual purpose. First, they support the handles when you wheel the cart. Second, they drop down and lock in place to support the cart in an upright position.

1. Cut the arms (K) to length. Mark the center of each end of each arm, measured from side to side. Measure down 3½"

from each end, and mark a point. Set the point of a compass at each of these points, and draw a 1¾"-radius semicircle at each end on both arms. Cut the curves with a jig saw.

2. Drill a 1"-dia. hole for the handle dowel at one of the centerpoints at the end of each arm. At the other centerpoint, drill a ⅜"-dia. guide hole for a carriage bolt.

Secure the wheels by inserting a cotter pin into a hole at the end of each axle, then bending the ends of the pin down with pliers.

ATTACH THE WHEELS.

Make sure to buy a steel axle rod that fits the holes in the hubs of the 10" wheels.

1. Cut the axle rod to 30" in length with a hacksaw. Remove any burrs with a file or bench grinder. (Rough-grit sandpaper also works, but it takes longer and is harder on the hands.) Secure the axle rod in a vise, or clamp it to your work surface, and use a steel twist bit to drill a ³⁄₁₆"-dia. hole through the rod ⅛" in from each end of the axle.

2. Slip the axle through the ½"-dia. holes drilled at the joints between the front and back supports. Slide two washers over each end of the axle.

3. Slip a wheel over each axle end, add two washers and insert ³⁄₁₆"-dia. cotter pins into the holes drilled at the ends of the axle. Secure the wheels by bending down the ends of the cotter pins with a pair of pliers **(photo G).**

LOCK THE ARMS IN PLACE.

1. On a flat surface, fold down the arm/handle assembly so the arms are perpendicular to the ground. Drill a ⅜"-dia. guide hole through each back support, 1" below the carriage bolt that attaches the arms to the supports. Extend the holes all the way through the arms **(photo H).** Insert a ⅜"-dia. hitch pin (or hinge pin) into each hole to secure the arms.

2. To avoid losing the pins when you remove them, attach them to the back supports with a chain or a piece of cord. Now, remove the pins and lift the arms so they are level with the tops of the back supports. Drill ⅜"-dia. holes through the arms and back supports, about 12" behind the first pin holes, for locking the arms in the cart-pushing position.

APPLY FINISHING TOUCHES.

Smooth out all the sharp edges on the cart with a sander. Also sand the surfaces slightly. Apply two coats of exterior wood stain to the wood for protection. Squirt some penetrating/lubricating oil or synthetic lubricant on the axle on each side of the wheels to reduce friction.

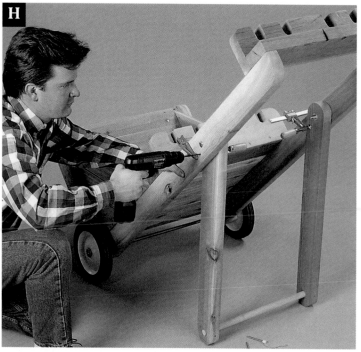

Drill ⅜"-dia. holes through the back supports and into the arms for inserting the hitch pins that lock the arms in position.

Cabin Marker

Hidden driveways and remote roads won't escape first-time visitors if they are marked with a striking, personalized cabin marker.

PROJECT
POWER TOOLS

Trips to a friend's cabin or vacation home, though usually enjoyable, often start on a confusing note. "Do you have the address written down?" is a common refrain after the fourth left into a dead end in the woods. You can save your friends confusion and wasted time by displaying your name, address and mailbox at the head of your driveway. And on a safety note, emergency vehicles can spot your home more quickly with a well-marked name and address on it.

The simple design of this cabin marker and mailbox stand makes it suitable for almost any yard. Its height ensures a certain level of prominence, but the cedar material and basic construction allow it to fit right in with its natural surroundings.

One of the best features of the cabin marker may be the least noticed—the base section. The base is a multi-tiered pyramid of 4 × 4 cedar timbers. It provides ample weight and stability, so you won't need to go to the trouble of digging a hole or pouring concrete. Just position the marker wherever you want it, and stake it in place. Much more attractive than a simple mailbox stand, this project will provide just the touch of originality that your cabin or vacation home deserves.

CONSTRUCTION MATERIALS

Quantity	Lumber
1	1 × 6" × 8' cedar
1	2 × 2" × 6' cedar
4	2 × 4" × 8' cedar
3	4 × 4" × 8' cedar

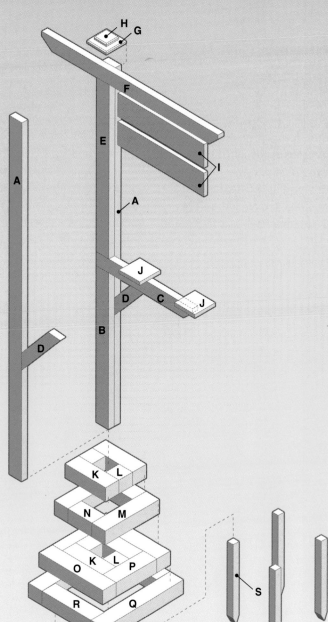

OVERALL SIZE:
85¾" HIGH
48½" WIDE
22" DEEP

Cutting List

Key	Part	Dimension	Pcs.	Material
A	Post side	1½ × 3½ × 84"	2	Cedar
B	Post section	1½ × 3½ × 36½"	1	Cedar
C	Mailbox arm	1½ × 3½ × 23½"	1	Cedar
D	Mailbox brace	1½ × 3½ × 17½"	2	Cedar
E	Post section	1½ × 3½ × 40½"	1	Cedar
F	Sign arm	1½ × 3½ × 48½"	1	Cedar
G	Top plate	⅞ × 5½ × 5½"	1	Cedar
H	Cap	⅞ × 3½ × 3½"	1	Cedar
I	Sign board	⅞ × 5½ × 24"	2	Cedar
J	Mailbox cleat	⅞ × 5½ × 5⅞"	2	Cedar

Cutting List

Key	Part	Dimension	Pcs.	Material
K	Base piece	3½ × 3½ × 10½"	4	Cedar
L	Base piece	3½ × 3½ × 4½"	4	Cedar
M	Base piece	3½ × 3½ × 15"	2	Cedar
N	Base piece	3½ × 3½ × 7"	2	Cedar
O	Base piece	3½ × 3½ × 17½"	2	Cedar
P	Base piece	3½ × 3½ × 11½"	2	Cedar
Q	Base piece	3½ × 3½ × 22"	2	Cedar
R	Base piece	3½ × 3½ × 14"	2	Cedar
S	Stake	1½ × 1½ × 18"	4	Cedar

Materials: Moisture-resistant glue, epoxy glue, 2", 2½" and 4" deck screws, #10 screw eyes (8), S-hooks (4),
⅜"-dia. × 5" galvanized lag screws with 1" washers (8), finishing materials.
Note: Measurements reflect the actual size of dimension lumber.

Directions: Cabin Marker

MAKE THE POST.

The post is made in three layers. Two post sections and two arms form the central layer, which is sandwiched between two post sides. The arms extend out from the post to support a mailbox and an address sign.

1. Cut the mailbox arm (C) and sign arm (F) to length. One end of the mailbox arm and both ends of the sign arm are cut with decorative slants on their bottom edges. To cut the ends of the arms to shape, mark a point on the three ends, 1" down from a long edge. On the opposite long edge, mark a point on the face 2½" in from the end. Draw a straight line connecting the points, and cut along it.

2. Cut the post sides (A) and post sections (B, E) to length. To assemble the post, you will sandwich the sections and the arms between the sides. Set one of the post sides on a flat work surface, and position the lower post section (B) on top of it, face to face, with the ends flush. Attach the lower post section to the side with wood glue and 2½" deck screws.

3. Position the mailbox arm on the side, making sure the square end is flush with the edge of the side. Use a square to make sure the mailbox arm is perpendicular to the side. Attach the mailbox arm, using glue and 2½" deck screws.

4. Butt the end of the upper post section (E) against the top edge of the mailbox arm, and attach it to the side in the same manner **(photo A).**

5. Position the sign arm at the top of the assembly so it extends 30" past the post on the side with the mailbox arm. Attach the sign arm to the post side with glue and deck screws.

6. Apply glue to the remaining side. Attach it to the post sections with glue and 4" deck screws, making sure all the ends are flush.

ATTACH THE MAILBOX CLEATS AND BRACES.

The cleats on the mailbox arm

Butt an end of the upper section against the top edge of the mailbox arm, and fasten it to the side.

Position a mailbox brace on each side of the mailbox arm, and fasten them to the post and arm.

Apply glue to the bottom face of the cap, and center it on the top of the post.

provide a stable nailing surface for a "rural-style" mailbox. The mailbox braces fasten to the post and mailbox arm to provide support.

1. Cut the mailbox cleats (J) to length and sand smooth. Center the cleats on the top of the mailbox arm. The frontmost cleat should overhang the front of the mailbox arm by 1". Center the remaining cleat 12½" in from the front of the mailbox arm. Attach the cleats with glue and 2½" deck screws.

2. Cut the mailbox braces (D) to length. Their ends must be cut at an angle. Use a power miter box, or a backsaw and miter box, to miter-cut each end of each mailbox brace at a 45° angle. Make sure the cuts at either end slant toward each other (see *Diagram,* page 49).

3. Position a mailbox brace against the side of the mailbox arm so one end is flush with the top edge of the mailbox arm and the other rests squarely against the post. Drill ⅛" pilot holes. Counterbore the holes ¼" deep, using a counterbore bit. Attach the mailbox braces with glue and 2½" deck screws **(photo B).**

COMPLETE THE POST TOP.

The post assembly is capped with a post top and cap made of 1" dimension lumber.

1. Cut the top plate (G) and cap (H) to size. Using a power sander, make ¼"-wide × ¼"-deep bevels along the top edges of the top and cap.

2. Center the top on the post, and attach it with glue and 2" deck screws. Center the cap on the top and attach it **(photo C).**

MAKE THE BASE.

The base for the cabin marker is made from cedar frames that increase in size from top to bottom. The frames are stacked to create a four-level pyramid. A fifth frame fits inside one of the frames to make a stabilizer for the post. The bottom frame is fastened to stakes driven into the ground to provide a secure anchor that does not require digging holes and pouring concrete footings.

1. Cut the 4 × 4 base pieces (K, L, M, N, O, P, Q, R) to length for all five frames. Assemble them into five frames according to the *Diagram,* page 49. To join the pieces, use 4" deck screws driven into pilot holes that have been counterbored 1½" deep.

2. After all five frames are built, join one of the small frames and the two next-smallest frames together in a pyramid, using glue and 4" deck screws **(photo D).** Insert the other small frame into the opening in the third-smallest frame. Secure with deck screws.

3. Set the base assembly on top of the large frame; do not attach them. Insert the post into the opening, and secure it with lag screws, driven through the top frame and into the post. (NOTE: The bottom frame is anchored to the ground on site before being attached to the pyramid.)

MAKE THE SIGN BOARDS.

1. Cut the sign boards (I) to size. Sand them smooth.

2. Stencil your name and address onto the signs. Or, you can use adhesive letters, freehand painting, a router with a veining bit or a woodburner. Be sure to test the technique on a sanded scrap of cedar before working on the signs.

Attach the base tiers to each other, working from top to bottom.

APPLY FINISHING TOUCHES.

1. Join the two signs together with #10 screw eyes and S-hooks. Drill pilot holes for the screw eyes in the sign arm and signs. Apply epoxy glue to the threads of the screws before inserting them. Apply your finish of choice.

2. Position the bottom frame of the base in the desired location. The area should be flat and level so the post is plumb. Check the frame with a level. Add or remove dirt around the base to achieve a level base before installing.

3. Cut the stakes (S) to length, and sharpen one end of each stake. Set the stakes in the inside corners of the frame. Drive them into the ground until the tops are lower than the tops of the frame. Attach the stakes to the frames with 4" deck screws.

4. Center the cabin marker on the bottom frame. Complete the base by driving 5" lag screws through the tops of the base into the bottom frame.

Cabin Porter

*Shuttle heavy supplies from car to cabin or down to your dock
with this smooth-riding cedar cart.*

Transporting luggage and supplies doesn't need to be an awkward, back-breaking exercise. Simply roll this cabin porter to your car when you arrive, load it up and wheel your gear to your cabin door or down to the dock. The porter is spacious enough to hold coolers, laundry baskets or grocery bags, all in one easy, convenient trip. Both end gates are removable, so you can transport longer items like skis, ladders or lumber for improvement projects. The cabin porter is also handy for moving heavy objects around your yard. The 10" wheels ensure a stable ride, and the porter is designed to minimize the chances of tipping. The wheels, axle and mounting hardware generally can be purchased as a set from a well-stocked hardware store. For winter use, you might try adding short skis or sled runners, allowing the cabin porter to glide over deep snow and decreasing your chances of dropping an armful of supplies over slippery ice.

CONSTRUCTION MATERIALS

Quantity	Lumber
3	2 × 4" × 8' cedar
11	1 × 4" × 8' cedar

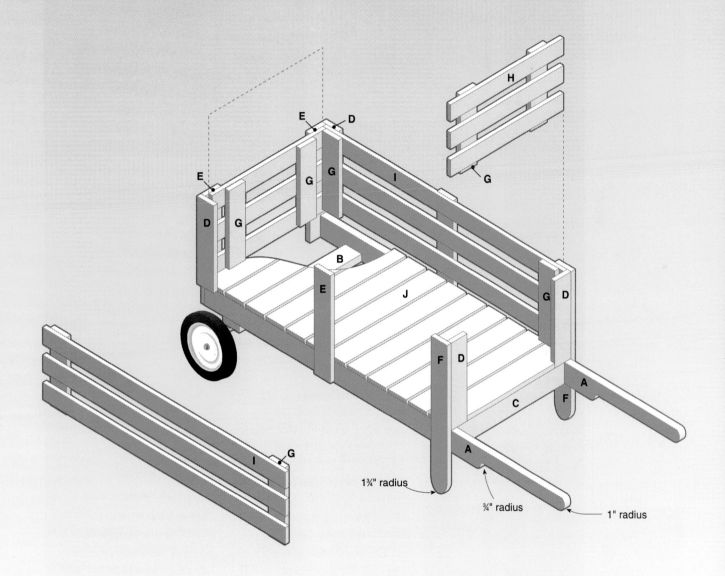

1¾" radius

¾" radius

1" radius

	Cutting List			
Key	**Part**	**Dimension**	**Pcs.**	**Material**
A	Handle	1½ × 3½ × 72⅞"	2	Cedar
B	Front stringer	1½ × 3½ × 24"	1	Cedar
C	Rear stringer	1½ × 3½ × 21"	1	Cedar
D	Short stile	⅞ × 3½ × 14⅜"	4	Cedar
E	Long stile	⅞ × 3½ × 17⅞"	4	Cedar

	Cutting List			
Key	**Part**	**Dimension**	**Pcs.**	**Material**
F	Rear stile	⅞ × 3½ × 24½"	2	Cedar
G	Gate stile	⅞ × 3½ × 13½"	8	Cedar
H	Gate rail	⅞ × 3½ × 22"	6	Cedar
I	Side rail	⅞ × 3½ × 46⅝"	6	Cedar
J	Slat	⅞ × 3½ × 24"	12	Cedar

Materials: 1½", 2", 2½" deck screws, wood glue, 10"-dia. wheels (2), axle, ¾ × 4" metal straps (3), ¼ × 1" lag screws, washers, crimp caps, finishing materials.
Note: Measurements reflect the actual size of dimension lumber.

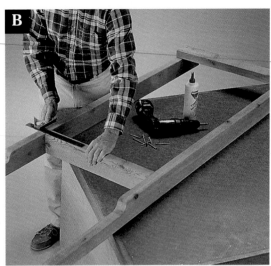

Clamp the handles together and draw reference lines at the stringer locations.

When installing the stringers, make sure they are square with the handles.

Directions:
Cabin Porter

ASSEMBLE THE HANDLES AND FRAMEWORK.
The framework for the cabin porter consists of handles connected by stringers at each end.
1. Cut the handles (A), front stringer (B) and rear stringer (C) to length. Sand the edges smooth.
2. Trim the back ends of the handles to create gripping surfaces. Draw a 16"-long cutting line on the face of each handle,

Apply glue and drive screws through the rails and into the corner pieces.

starting at one end, 1½" up from the bottom edge. Set the point of a compass at the bottom edge, 14½" in from the end, and draw a 1½"-radius arc, creating a smooth curve leading up to the cut line. To round the ends of each handle, use a compass to draw a 1"-radius semicircle centered 1" below the top edge and 1" in from the end (see *Diagram,* page 53). Shape the handles by cutting with a jig saw, then sand the edges smooth.
3. Stringers and slats fit across the handles, creating the bottom frame of the porter. Clamp the handles together, edge to edge, so the ends are flush, and draw reference lines 25⅜" from the grip ends and 3½" from the square ends to locate the stringers **(photo A).** Place the front stringer flat across the bottom edges of the handles so the front edge of the stringer is flush with the 3½" reference lines. Attach it with glue and 2½" deck screws. Position the rear stringer between the handles so the back face of the stringer is flush with the 25⅜" reference lines. Attach it

with glue and 2½" deck screws **(photo B).**
4. Cut the slats (J) to length, and round over their top edges with a sander.
5. Position the handle assembly so the shaped grip edges face down. Lay one slat over the handles at the front end so the corners of the slat are flush with the ends of the handles. Drill ⅛" pilot holes through the slat, and counterbore the holes to a ¼" depth. Fasten the slat with glue and 2" deck screws.
6. Notch the rear end slat to receive the rear short stiles. Draw lines at both ends of the slat ⅞" from a common long edge and 3½" from the ends. Cut the notches with a jig saw. Position the slat flush with the rear face of the rear stringer, and fasten it with glue and 2" screws.
7. Space the remaining slats evenly between the end slats with gaps of about ½". Fasten them with glue and 2" screws.

MAKE THE CORNERS.
Join the stiles to make the corners, which will support the side rails and end gates.
1. Cut the short stiles (D), long

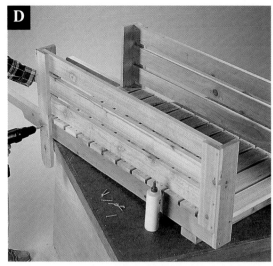

Anchor the sides to the framework with glue and screws driven through the stiles into the handles.

Attach the axles to the bottom of the front stringer with metal straps fastened with lag screws.

stiles (E) and rear stiles (F) to length. Use a compass to draw a 1¾"-radius semicircle at the bottom of each rear stile (see *Diagram*, page 53). Shape the ends with a jig saw, and sand the edges smooth.

2. Butt the edge of a short stile against the face of a rear stile so the pieces form a right angle. With the square ends flush, drill pilot holes every 2" through the rear stile and into the edge of the short stile. Counterbore the holes. Join the stiles with glue and 2" deck screws. Assemble the other rear corner.

3. Repeat this procedure to assemble the front corners, butting the edge of a long stile against the face of a short stile so the edges and tops are flush.

MAKE THE SIDES.

1. Cut the side rails (I) to length. Place three side rails tight between one front corner and one rear corner so the top of the upper rail is flush with the tops of the corners. Leave a 1" gap between rails. Fasten the rails to the corners with glue and 1½" deck screws **(photo C).**

2. Fasten the side assemblies to the handles with glue and 2" deck screws **(photo D).** Drive an additional screw through each stile and into the edge of an adjacent slat. Position the remaining stiles (E) on the outer sides of the rails, midway between the front and rear corners. Fasten the stiles to the rails with glue and 1½" deck screws.

MAKE THE GATES.

1. Cut the gate stiles (G) and gate rails (H) to length. Sand the short edges of the rails.

2. Lay the rails facedown together in groups of three with the ends flush. Draw reference lines across the rails 2" in from each end to locate the stiles.

3. Place two stiles on one rail with the tops flush and the outer stile edges on the reference lines. Fasten them with glue and 1½" deck screws driven through the stiles and into the rails.

4. Attach two more rails below the first one, leaving a 1" gap between the rails.

5. Follow the same procedure to make the other gate.

6. Set the gates in place be-

tween the porter sides to locate the four remaining gate stiles (G). These form the slots that keep the gates in place. Position the stiles flush with the tops of the top side rails and almost flush with the faces of the gate rails. Attach them with glue and 1½" deck screws driven through the stiles and into the rails. Slide the gates in and out of the slots to test for smooth operation.

7. Sand any rough areas, and apply the finish of your choice.

ATTACH THE WHEELS.

1. Cut the axle to length (24" plus the width of the two wheels plus 1½"). Attach the axle to the bottom of the front stringer with lag screws and metal straps bent in the center **(photo E).** Place one strap at each end of the stringer and one in the middle.

2. Slide three washers followed by a wheel over each end of the axle. Secure the wheels with crimp caps or by drilling a small hole in each end of the axle and installing an additional washer and a cotter pin.

Porch Swing

*You'll cherish the pleasant memories created
by this porch swing built for two.*

CONSTRUCTION MATERIALS

Quantity	Lumber
10	1 × 2" × 8' pine
1	1 × 4" × 4' pine
2	2 × 4" × 10' pine
1	2 × 6" × 10' pine

Nothing conjures up pleasant images of a cool summer evening like a porch swing. When the porch swing is one that you've built yourself, those evenings will be all the more pleasant. This porch swing is made from sturdy pine to provide years and years of memory making. The gentle curve of the slatted seat and the relaxed angle of the swing back are designed for your comfort. When you build your porch swing, pay close attention to the spacing of the rope holes drilled in the back, arms and seat of the swing. They are arranged to create perfect balance when you hang your swing from your porch ceiling.

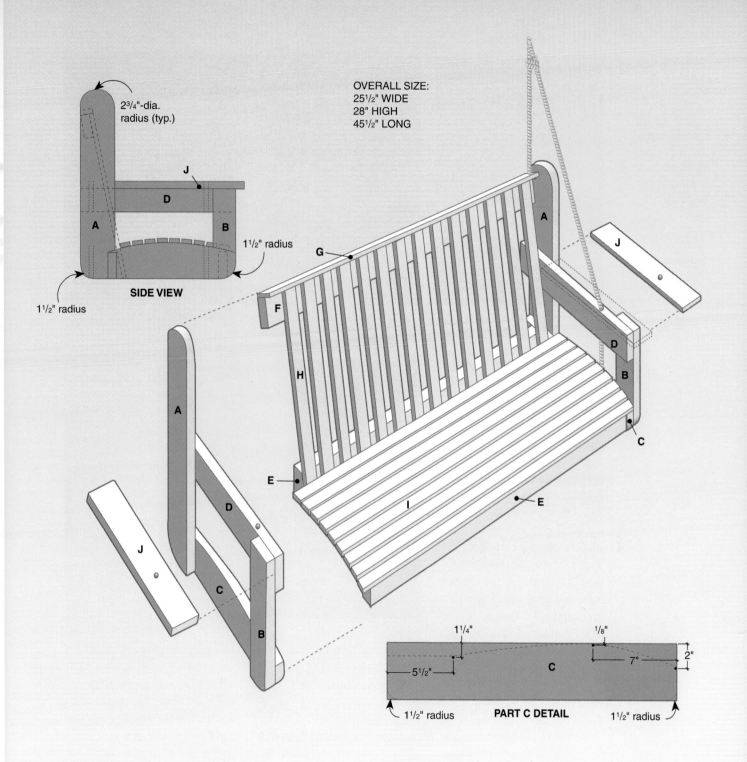

$2^3/_4$"-dia.
radius (typ.)

OVERALL SIZE:
$25^1/_2$" WIDE
28" HIGH
$45^1/_2$" LONG

SIDE VIEW

$1^1/_2$" radius

$1^1/_2$" radius

J

D

A

B

G

F

H

A

E

A

D

B

C

I

E

D

B

C

J

J

PART C DETAIL

$1^1/_4$"

$1/_8$"

2"

$5^1/_2$"

7"

C

$1^1/_2$" radius

$1^1/_2$" radius

Cutting List				
Key	**Part**	**Dimension**	**Pcs.**	**Material**
A	Back upright	$1^1/_2 \times 5^1/_2 \times 28$"	2	Pine
B	Front upright	$1^1/_2 \times 3^1/_2 \times 13^1/_2$"	2	Pine
C	Seat support	$1^1/_2 \times 5^1/_2 \times 24$"	2	Pine
D	Arm rail	$1^1/_2 \times 3^1/_2 \times 24$"	2	Pine
E	Stretcher	$1^1/_2 \times 3^1/_2 \times 39$"	2	Pine

Cutting List				
Key	**Part**	**Dimension**	**Pcs.**	**Material**
F	Back cleat	$1^1/_2 \times 3^1/_2 \times 42$"	1	Pine
G	Top rail	$^3/_4 \times 1^1/_2 \times 42$"	1	Pine
H	Back slat	$^3/_4 \times 1^1/_2 \times 25$"	14	Pine
I	Seat slat	$^3/_4 \times 1^1/_2 \times 42$"	9	Pine
J	Arm rest	$^3/_4 \times 3^1/_2 \times 20$"	2	Pine

Materials: Moisture-resistant glue, $1/_2$"-dia. nylon rope (20'), #8 x 2", #10 x $2^1/_2$" and #10 x 3" wood screws.

Note: Measurements reflect the actual size of dimension lumber.

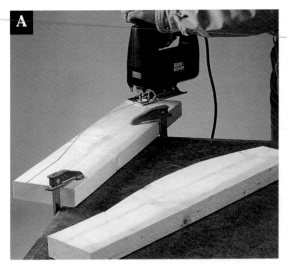

Use a jig saw to cut the contours into the tops of the seat supports.

Use a ⅝" spade bit and a right-angle drilling guide when drilling rope holes through the seat supports.

Directions: Porch Swing

MAKE THE SEAT SUPPORTS.
1. Cut the seat supports (C) to length. Using the pattern on page 57 as a guide, lay out the contour on one of the seat supports. Use a flexible ruler, bent to follow the contour, to ensure a smooth cutting line.
2. Cut along the cutting line with a jig saw **(photo A).** Sand the contour and round the bottom front edge with a belt sander. Use the contoured seat support as a template to mark, cut and sand a matching contour on the other seat support.

BUILD THE SEAT FRAME.
1. Cut the arm rails (D) and stretchers (E) to length. Attach one stretcher between the seat supports, ¾" from the front edges and ½" from the bottom edges, using glue and 2½" wood screws. Fasten the other stretcher between the supports so the front face of the stretcher is 6" from the backs of the supports, and all bottom edges are flush.
2. Use a ⅝" spade bit and drill guide holes for the ropes through the seat supports and

Smooth out the top exposed edges of the seat slats with a router and ¼" roundover bit (or use a power sander).

the arm rails. Drill a hole 1½" from the back end of each piece. Also drill a hole 4½" from the front end of each piece. Use a right-angle drill guide to make sure holes stay centered all the way through **(photo B).**

INSTALL THE SEAT SLATS.
1. Cut the seat slats (I) to length (use full-sized 1 × 2s, not 1 × 2 furring strips). Arrange the slats across the seat supports, using ½"-thick spacers to make sure the gaps are even. The front slat should overhang the front stretcher by about ¼".
2. Fasten the slats to the seat

support with glue and #8 × 2" wood screws (one screw at each slat end). Do not attach the back slat until after you install the back assembly. Smooth the top edges of the slats with a router and ¼" roundover bit, or a power sander **(photo C).**

BUILD THE BACK.
1. Cut the back cleat (F) and the back slats (H) to length.
2. Fasten the slats to the back cleat, leaving a 1½" gap at each end, and spacing the slats at 1⅜" intervals **(photo D).** The tops of the slats should be flush with the top of the cleat.

Use 1⅜" spacers to align the back slats, then fasten the slats to the back cleat.

Fasten the top rail to the back cleat, so the front edge of the rail is flush with the fronts of the slats.

Slide the back assembly behind the seat assembly and attach.

3. Cut the top rail (G) to length. Fasten it to the cleat so the front edge of the rail is flush with the fronts of the slats **(photo E).**

ATTACH THE UPRIGHTS AND ARM REST.

1. Cut the back uprights (A) and front uprights (B). Make a round profile cut at the tops of the back uprights (see pattern, page 57), using a jig saw. Attach the uprights to the outside faces of the seat supports, flush with the ends of the supports, using glue and 2½" screws.

2. Round the bottom front corners of the front uprights and bottom rear corners of the back uprights with a sander, so they are flush with the seat supports.

3. Use 2½" screws to attach arm rails between the uprights, flush with the tops and with rope holes aligned.

4. Slide the back slat assembly behind the seat assembly **(photo F).** Attach the back cleat to the back uprights with 3" screws, so the upper rear corners of the cleat are flush with the back edges of the uprights, 3" down from the tops of the uprights. Make sure the back faces of the back slats are resting against the top front edge of the rear stretcher.

5. Attach the back seat slat to the seat supports, so its back edge is snug against the front faces of the back slats.

6. Cut and sand the arm rests (J) and set them on the arm rail, centered side to side and flush with the back uprights.

7. Mark the locations of the rope holes in the arm rails onto the arm rests. Drill matching holes into the arm rests. Attach the arm rests to the rails with glue and 2" screws.

APPLY FINISHING TOUCHES.

Sand and paint swing. Thread ½"-dia. nylon rope through the rope holes, and knot the ends. Hang the swing with heavy screw eyes driven into ceiling joists or into a 2 × 4 lag-screwed across the ceiling joists.

Compost Bin

Convert yard waste to garden fertilizer inside this simple and stylish cedar compost bin.

CONSTRUCTION MATERIALS

Quantity	Lumber
4	4 × 4" × 4' cedar posts
5	2 × 2" × 8' cedar
8	1 × 6" × 8' cedar fence boards

Composting yard debris is an increasingly popular practice that makes good environmental sense. Composting is the process of converting organic waste into rich fertilizer for the soil, usually in a compost bin. A well-designed compost bin has a few key features. It's big enough to contain the organic material as it decomposes. It allows cross-flow of air to speed the process. And the bin area is easy to reach whether you're adding waste, turning the compost or removing the composted material. This compost bin has all these features, plus one additional benefit not shared by most compost bins: it's very attractive.

OVERALL SIZE:
30" HIGH
40½" WIDE
48" LONG

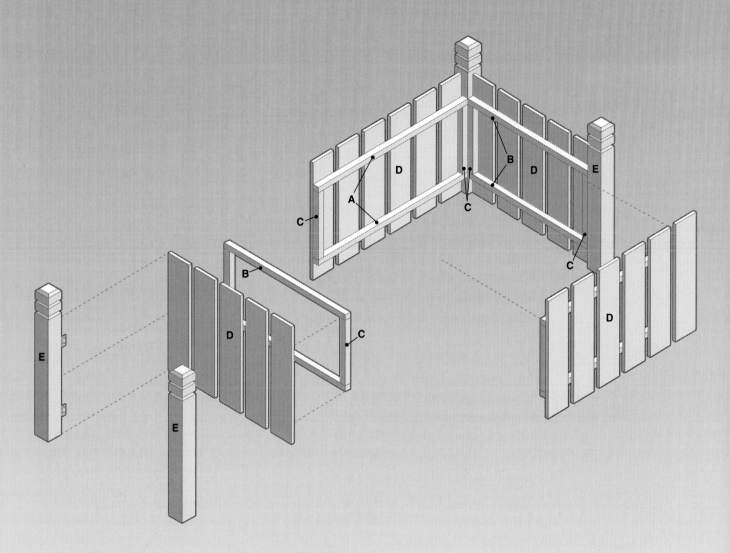

Cutting List

Key	Part	Dimension	Pcs.	Material
A	Side rail	1½ × 1½ × 40½"	4	Cedar
B	End rail	1½ × 1½ × 33½"	4	Cedar
C	Cleat	1½ × 1½ × 15"	8	Cedar
D	Slat	¾ × 5½ × 27"	22	Cedar
E	Post	3½ × 3½ × 30"	4	Cedar

Materials: 1½" and 3" galvanized deck screws, hook-and-eye latch mechanism, 3 × 3" brass butt hinges (one pair) and screws.

Note: Measurements reflect the actual size of dimension lumber.

Fasten the cleats between the rails to construct the panel frames.

Attach a slat at each end of the panel frame so the outer edges of the slats are flush with the outer edges of the frame.

Directions:
Compost Bin

BUILD THE PANELS.

The four fence-type panels that make up the sides of this compost bin are cedar slats that attach to panel frames. The panel frames for the front and back of the bin are longer than the frames for the sides.

1. Cut the side rails (A), end rails (B) and cleats (C) to length. Group pairs of matching rails with a pair of cleats. Assemble each group into a frame—the cleats should be between the rails, flush with the ends. Drill ⅛" pilot holes into the rails. Counterbore the holes ¼" deep, using a counterbore bit. Fasten all four panel frames together by driving 3" deck screws through the rails and into each end of each cleat **(photo A).**

2. Cut all of the slats (D) to length. Lay the frames on a flat surface and place a slat at each end of each frame. Keep the edges of these outer slats flush with the outside edges of the frame and let the bottoms of the slats overhang the bottom frame rail by 4". Drill pilot holes

in the slats. Counterbore the holes slightly. Fasten the outer slats to the frames with 1½" deck screws **(photo B).**

3. When you have fastened the outer slats to all of the frames, add slats between each pair of outer slats to fill out the panels. Insert a 1½" spacing block between the slats to set the correct gap. (This will allow air to flow into the bin.) Be sure to keep the ends of the slats

> **TIP**
>
> *Grass clippings, leaves, weeds and vegetable waste are some of the most commonly composted materials. Just about any formerly living organic material can be composted, but DO NOT add any of the following items to your compost bin:*
> *• animal material or waste*
> *• dairy products*
> *• papers with colored inks*
> *For more information on composting, contact your local library or agricultural extension office.*

aligned. Check with a tape measure to make sure the bottoms of all the slats are 4" below the bottom of the panel frame **(photo C).**

ATTACH THE PANELS AND POSTS.

The four slatted panels are joined with corner posts to make the bin. Three of the panels are attached permanently to the posts, while one of the end panels is installed with hinges and a latch so it can swing open like a gate. You can use plain 4 × 4 cedar posts for the corner posts. For a more decorative look, you can buy prefabricated fence posts or deck rail posts with carving or contours at the top.

1. Cut the posts (E) to length. If you're using plain posts, you may want to do some decorative contouring at one end or attach post caps.

2. Stand a post upright on a flat work surface. Set one of the longer slatted panels next to the post, resting on the bottoms of the slats. Hold or clamp the panel to the post, with the back of the panel frame flush with

The inner slats should be 1½" apart, with the ends 4" below the bottom of the frame.

Stand the posts and panels upright, and fasten the panels to the posts by driving screws through the cleats.

one of the faces of the post. Fasten the panel to the post by driving 3" deck screws through the frame cleats and into the posts. Space screws at roughly 8" intervals.

3. Stand another post on end, and fasten the other end of the panel frame to it, making sure the posts are aligned.

4. Fasten one of the shorter panels to the adjoining face of one of the posts. The back faces of the frames should just meet in a properly formed corner **(photo D).** Fasten another post at the free end of the shorter panel.

5. Fasten the other longer panel to the posts so it is opposite the first longer panel, forming a U-shaped structure.

ATTACH THE GATE.

The unattached shorter panel is attached at the open end of the bin with hinges to create a swinging gate for loading and unloading material. Exterior wood stain will keep the cedar from turning gray. If you are planning to apply a finish, you'll find it easier to apply it before you hang the gate. Make sure all hardware is rated for exterior use.

1. Set the last panel between the posts at the open end of the bin. Move the sides of the bin slightly, if needed, so there is about ¼" of clearance between each end of the panel and the posts. Remove this panel gate and attach a pair of 3" butt hinges to a cleat, making sure the barrels of the hinges extend past the face of the outer slats.

2. Set the panel into the opening, and mark the location of the hinge plates onto the post. Open the hinge so it is flat, and attach it to the post **(photo E).**

3. Attach a hook-and-eye latch to the unhinged end of the panel to hold the gate closed.

Attach the hinges to the end panel frame, then fasten to the post.

Dock Box

This spacious dockside hold protects all your boating supplies, with room to spare.

CONSTRUCTION MATERIALS

Quantity	Lumber
2	⅝" × 4 × 8' plywood siding
7	1 × 2" × 8' cedar
4	1 × 4" × 8' cedar
1	1 × 6" × 8' cedar
3	2 × 2" × 8' cedar

With its spacious storage compartment and appealing nautical design, this box is a perfect place for stowing water sports equipment. You won't have to haul gear inside anymore after offshore excursions. Life preservers, beach toys, ropes and even small coolers conveniently fit inside this attractive chest, which has ventilation holes to discourage mildew. Sturdy enough for seating, the large top can hold charts, fishing gear or a light snack while you await your next voyage. With a dock box to hold your gear, you can spend your energy carrying more important items—like the fresh catch of the day—up to your cabin.

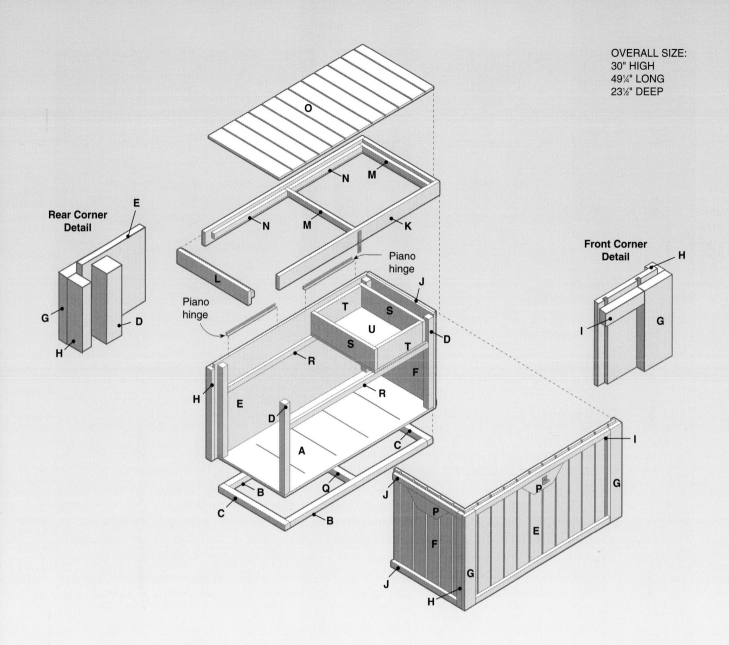

OVERALL SIZE:
30" HIGH
49¼" LONG
23½" DEEP

Rear Corner Detail

Front Corner Detail

Piano hinge

Piano hinge

		Cutting List		
Key	**Part**	**Dimension**	**Pcs.**	**Material**
A	Bottom	⅝ × 46¼ × 20½"	1	Plywood siding
B	Bottom brace	1½ × 1½ × 43¼"	2	Cedar
C	End brace	1½ × 1½ × 20½"	2	Cedar
D	Corner brace	1½ × 1½ × 24⅜"	4	Cedar
E	Large panel	⅝ × 47½ × 27"	2	Plywood siding
F	Small panel	⅝ × 20½ × 27"	2	Plywood siding
G	Corner trim	⅞ × 3½ × 26½"	4	Cedar
H	Corner batten	⅞ × 1½ × 26½"	4	Cedar
I	Long trim	⅞ × 1½ × 42¼"	4	Cedar
J	End trim	⅞ × 1½ × 18¾"	4	Cedar
K	Lid side	⅞ × 3½ × 49¼"	2	Cedar

		Cutting List		
Key	**Part**	**Dimension**	**Pcs.**	**Material**
L	Lid end	⅞ × 3½ × 21¾"	2	Cedar
M	Top support	⅞ × 1½ × 21¾"	3	Cedar
N	Ledger	⅞ × 1½ × 22⅜"	4	Cedar
O	Top panel	⅝ × 47½ × 21¾"	1	Plywood siding
P	Handle	⅞ × 3½ × 13½"	4	Cedar
Q	Cross brace	1½ × 1½ × 17½	1	Cedar
R	Tray slide	⅞ × 1½ × 43¼"	2	Cedar
S	Tray side	⅞ × 5½ × 20¼"	2	Cedar
T	Tray end	⅞ × 5½ × 14"	2	Cedar
U	Tray bottom	⅝ × 15¾ × 20¼"	1	Plywood siding

Materials: 1¼", 1⅝" deck screws, 6d finish nails, 1" wire brads, construction adhesive, 1½ × 30" or 36" piano hinge, hasp, lid support chains (2), finishing materials.

Note: Measurements reflect the actual size of dimension lumber.

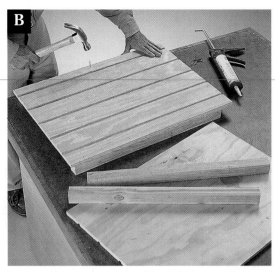

For ventilation, cut slots into the bottom panel, using a straightedge as a stop block for the foot of your circular saw.

Position the corner braces beneath the small panels, and fasten them with adhesive and finish nails.

Directions: Dock Box

MAKE THE BOX BOTTOM. The box bottom is made of grooved plywood siding attached to a rectangular 2 × 2 box frame.

1. Cut the bottom (A), bottom braces (B), end braces (C) and cross brace (Q) to size. Apply construction adhesive or moisture-resistant wood glue to the ends of the bottom braces. Clamp them between the end braces so the edges are flush. Drill ⅛" pilot holes through each end brace into the bottom braces. Counterbore the

Attach the corner trim pieces flush with the edges of the corner battens to cover the plywood joints.

holes ¼" deep, using a counterbore bit. Drive 1⅝" deck screws through the pilot holes to reinforce the joints.

2. Center the cross brace in the frame and attach it with adhesive and 1⅝" deck screws.

3. Attach the box bottom to the box frame with 1⅝" deck screws.

4. Cut six ventilation slots in the bottom panel. First, clamp a straightedge near one edge of the bottom panel. Then, set the cutting depth on your circular saw to about 1" and press the foot of the saw up against the straightedge. Turn on the saw, and press down with the blade in a rocking motion until

you've cut through the bottom panel **(photo A).** The slots should be spaced evenly, 8" to 9" apart.

ATTACH THE BOX SIDES.
1. Cut the corner braces (D), large panels (E) and small panels (F) to size. Align two corner braces under a small panel (grooved side up). Make sure the edges are flush, with a ½"-wide gap at one end of the panel and a 2⅛"-wide gap at the other end. Fasten the braces with construction adhesive and 6d finish nails **(photo B).**

2. Repeat the procedure for the other small panel.

3. Attach the small panels, with the 2" space facing downward, to the end braces, using 6d nails and construction adhesive.

4. Place the large panels in position and drive nails through the panels into the bottom braces and corner braces.

MAKE THE TRIM PIECES.
1. Cut the corner trim (G) and corner battens (H) to length. Set the project on its side. Use construction adhesive and nails to attach the corner bat-

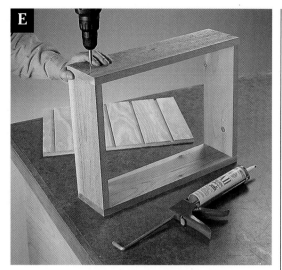

A handle block is attached to each face of the box, up against the bottom of the top trim piece.

Counterbore the screw heads so they don't obstruct the movement of the tray on the tray slides.

tens flush with the bottom, covering the seam between panels. There should be a ½"-wide gap between the tops of the corner pieces and the top of the box. Then, attach the corner trim **(photo C)**.

2. Cut the long trim (I) and the end trim (J) to length. Attach the lower trim flush with the bottom, using construction adhesive and finish nails.

3. Attach the upper trim pieces flush with the corner pieces, using adhesive. Drive 1¼" deck screws from inside the box into the trim pieces.

ATTACH THE HANDLES.

The handles (P) are trapezoid-shaped blocks cut from cedar.

1. Cut four handles to length. Mark each piece 3¾" in from each end along one long edge. Connect the marks diagonally to the adjacent corners to form cutting lines. Cut with a circular saw or a power miter box.

2. Center a handle against the bottom edge of the top trim piece on each face. Attach each handle with adhesive and 1¼" deck screws **(photo D)**.

MAKE THE TRAY.

The tray rests inside the dock box on slides.

1. Cut the tray slides (R) to length. Mount the slides inside the box, 7" down from the top edge, using adhesive and 1¼" deck screws.

2. Cut the tray sides (S), tray ends (T) and tray bottom (U) to size. Drill pilot holes in the tray ends and counterbore the holes. Then, fasten the tray ends between the tray sides with adhesive and 1⅝" deck screws **(photo E)**. Attach the tray bottom with adhesive and 1" wire brads.

MAKE THE LID.

1. Cut the lid sides (K) and lid ends (L) to length. Fasten them together with adhesive and drive 6d nails through the lid sides and into the ends.

2. Cut the top panel (O), top supports (M) and ledgers (N) to length. Attach two top supports to the inside edges of the frame, ⅝" down from the top edge, using adhesive and 1¼" screws **(photo F)**. Attach the ledgers to the long sides of the lid—one at each corner—with

adhesive and 1¼" deck screws. Place the remaining top support into the gap in the middle. Fasten it by driving 6d nails into the ends of the support.

3. Fit the top panel into the lid. Fasten with 6d nails and adhesive. Sand all exposed edges.

4. Attach the lid to the box with a piano hinge cut in two. Attach a pair of chains between the bottom of the lid and the front of the box to hold the lid upright when open. To lock the box, attach a hasp to the handle and lid at the front of the box.

5. Apply exterior stain or water sealer for protection. Caulk the gap around the top panel and lid frame with exterior caulk.

Top supports in the lid frame support the top panel.

Grill Garage

*Eliminate mess and clutter and shelter grilling appliances
from the elements with this spacious grill garage.*

CONSTRUCTION MATERIALS

Quantity	Lumber
2	½" × 4 × 8' textured cedar sheet siding
1	¾" × 2 × 2' plywood
10	1 × 2" × 8' cedar

Summer cookouts will be more enjoyable with this handy grill garage and storage unit. Unlike most prefabricated grill garages, this project is sized to store today's popular gas grills, as well as traditional charcoal grills. And while you're using your grill, the spacious top platforms of the grill garage can be used as convenient staging and serving areas. The walls of this grill garage are made from inexpensive, attractive rough cedar siding panels. Fitted with a cabinet-style door, the storage compartment can accommodate two large bags of charcoal, plus all your grilling accessories.

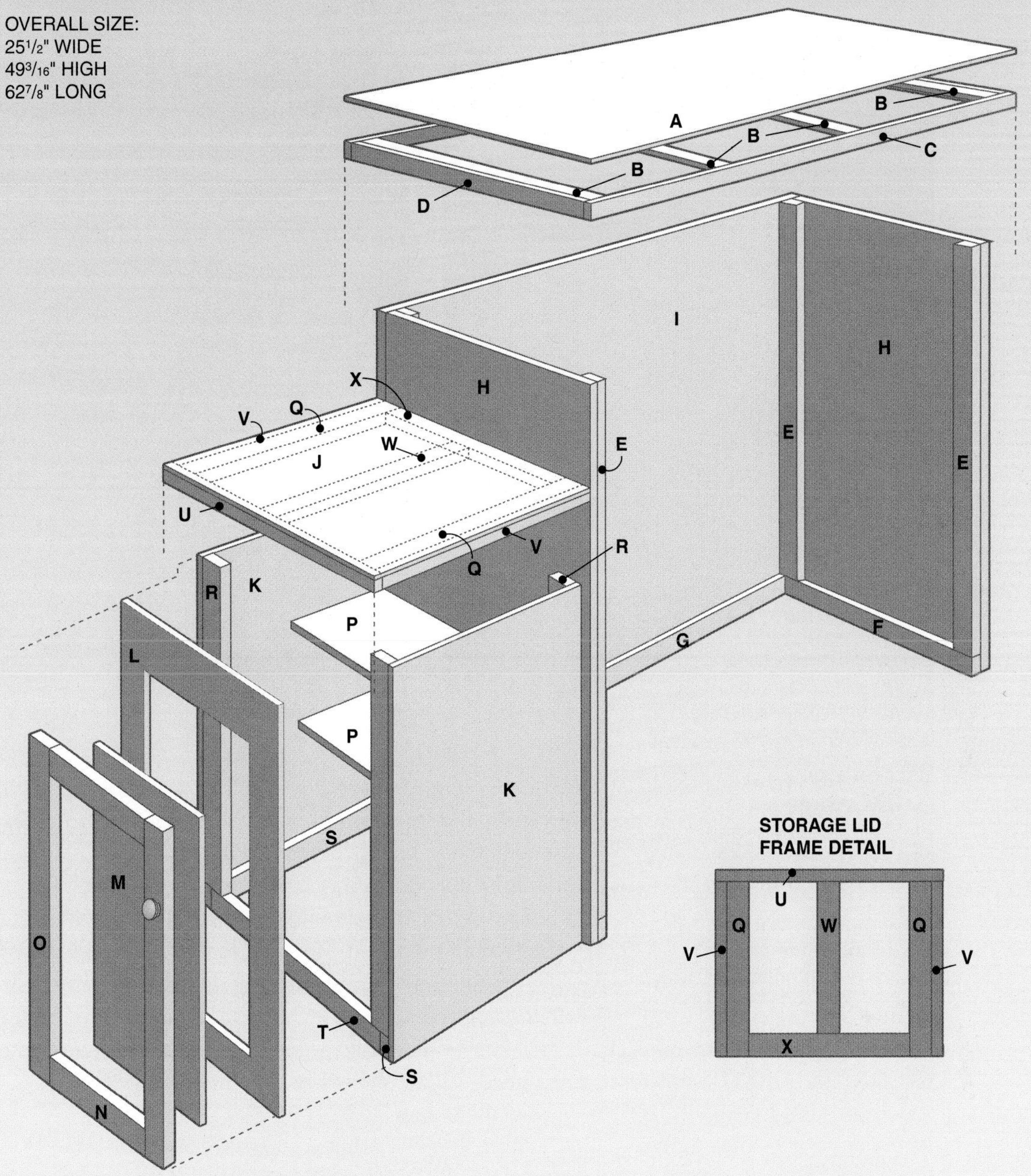
OVERALL SIZE:
25 1/2" WIDE
49 3/16" HIGH
62 7/8" LONG
A
B
B
B
C
D
I
H
H
X
V
Q
W
J
E
E
E
U
V
Q
R
R
K
P
P
K
G
F
L
S
M
O
T
S
N
STORAGE LID FRAME DETAIL
U
Q
W
Q
V
V
X

Cutting List

Key	Part	Dimension	Pcs.	Material
A	Garage lid	7/16 × 25½ × 43⅝"	1	Cedar siding
B	Lid stringer	¾ × 1½ × 24"	4	Cedar
C	Lid-frame side	¾ × 1½ × 43⅝"	2	Cedar
D	Lid-frame end	¾ × 1½ × 24"	2	Cedar
E	Posts	¾ × 1½ × 46½"	4	Cedar
F	End plate	¾ × 1½ × 22 13/16"	2	Cedar
G	Back plate	¾ × 1½ × 41¼"	1	Cedar
H	End panel	7/16 × 23 9/16 × 48"	2	Cedar siding
I	Back panel	7/16 × 42⅛ × 48"	1	Cedar siding
J	Storage lid	7/16 × 20 × 24"	1	Cedar siding
K	Side panel	7/16 × 19¼ × 29¼"	2	Cedar siding
L	Face panel	7/16 × 22½ × 29¼"	1	Cedar siding

Cutting List

Key	Part	Dimension	Pcs.	Material
M	Door panel	7/16 × 18½ × 23¼"	1	Cedar siding
N	Door rail	¾ × 1½ × 17"	2	Cedar
O	Door stile	¾ × 1½ × 24¾"	2	Cedar
P	Shelf	¾ × 10 × 21⅜"	2	Plywood
Q	End stringer	¾ × 1½ × 19¼"	2	Cedar
R	Short post	¾ × 1½ × 27¾"	4	Cedar
S	Side plate	¾ × 1½ × 19¼"	2	Cedar
T	Front plate	¾ × 1½ × 20⅛"	1	Cedar
U	Front lid edge	¾ × 1½ × 24"	1	Cedar
V	Storage lid end	¾ × 1½ × 19¼"	2	Cedar
W	Center stringer	¾ × 1½ × 17¾"	1	Cedar
X	Rear lid edge	¾ × 1½ × 19½"	1	Cedar

Materials: Moisture-resistant glue, 1", 1½", 2" and 3" deck screws, hinges, door pull, finishing materials.

Note: Measurements reflect actual size of dimension lumber.

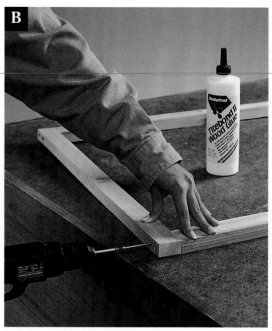

Install stringers inside the garage-lid frame to strengthen the garage lid.

Use 1 × 2 posts to create the framework for the main garage compartment.

Directions: Grill Garage

MAKE THE GARAGE LID PANEL.

1. Cut the garage lid (A) to size. (Use a straightedge cutting guide whenever cutting sheet goods.) Cut the lid stringers (B), lid-frame sides (C) and lid-frame ends (D) to length. On a flat work surface, arrange the frame ends and sides on edge to form the lid frame. Fasten the lid sides and lid ends together with glue. Drive 1½" deck screws through the sides and into the ends of the lid-frame ends.

2. Position the lid stringers facedown in the frame, with one on each end and two spaced evenly in between. Attach the stringers and frame with glue and 1½" deck screws **(photo A)**.

3. Turn the frame over so the side where the stringers are flush with the top edges of the frame is facing up. Lay the garage lid on top of the frame assembly and test the fit—the edges of the lid should be flush with the edges of the frame.

4. Remove the garage lid and run a bead of glue on the top edges of the frame. Drill ⅛" pilot holes in the lid. Counterbore the holes ¼" deep, using a counterbore bit. Reposition the lid on the frame assembly. Drive 1" deck screws through the lid and into the tops of the frame components.

BUILD THE GARAGE WALLS.

1. Cut the posts (E) and end plates (F) to length. Cut the end panels (H) to size. Assemble an end plate and two posts into an open-end frame on your work surface. Fasten the parts together with glue. Drive 1½" deck screws through

the end plate and into the ends of the posts **(photo B)**.

2. Test the fit. Drill pilot holes in the end panel. Counterbore the holes. Attach an end panel to the frame with glue. Drive 1" deck screws through the panel and into the frame **(photo C)**.

3. Build the other end panel the same way.

ASSEMBLE THE GARAGE PANELS.

1. Cut the back plate (G) to length. Cut the back panel (I) to size.

2. Stand one end-panel assembly up so it rests on the plate. Place a bead of glue along the edge of the post that will join the back panel. Position one end of the back panel flush against the post, making sure the rough side of the cedar siding is facing out. Attach the back panel to the end-panel assembly with 1½" screws. Attach the other end-panel assembly to the other side of the back

Attach the end panel to the open-ended frame assembly, making sure that the rough side of the cedar siding is facing outward.

panel the same way **(photo D)**.
3. Place a bead of glue along the outside face of the back plate. Position the plate at the bottom of the back panel, so the ends of the plate form butt joints with the end-panel assemblies. Secure by driving 1" deck screws through the back panel and into the back plate.
4. Fit the garage lid panel around the tops of the end and back panels, shifting the panels slightly to create a tight fit. Drill pilot holes in the lid frame. Counterbore the holes. Attach the lid panel with glue. Drive 2" deck screws through the lid frame and into the tops of the end and back panels and frame posts.

BUILD THE CABINET LID.

1. Cut the storage lid (J) to size. Cut the end stringers (Q), center stringer (W), front lid edge (U), rear lid edge (X) and storage lid ends (V) to length.
2. Lay the two storage lid ends

and the front lid edge on edge on a flat surface. Position the storage lid ends so that they butt into the back face of the front lid edge. Fasten the ends and edge together with glue and 1½" deck screws.
3. Lay the rear lid edge on its face between the end stringers, which are facedown, flush with the ends of the stringers. Mounting the rear lid edge in this way provides a flush fit at the rear of the storage unit assembly while maintaining an overhang on the sides and front. Fasten the rear lid edge and end stringers together with glue and 3" deck screws.
4. Fasten the storage-lid end/edge assembly to the end

stringer/rear-lid edge assembly with glue and 3" deck screws to form a frame. Position the center stringer midway between the end stringers and attach with glue and 3" deck screws.
5. Turn the storage lid frame over so the side with the stringers flush with the tops of the frame faces up. Lay the storage lid panel on top of the frame so the edges are flush. Drill pilot holes in the lid and counterbore the holes. Attach the lid panel with glue and drive 1" deck screws through the panel and into the frame.

BUILD THE CABINET WALLS.

1. Cut the short posts (R) and side plates (S) to length. Cut the side panels (K) to size.
2. Attach a side plate to the bottom, inside edge of a side panel, so the plate is flush with the front edge of the panel **(photo E).** Attach the short

Attach the back panel to the posts of the end panels to assemble the walls of the main grill garage compartment.

Attact the side plate, with the face against the panel, to the bottom edge of the side panel.

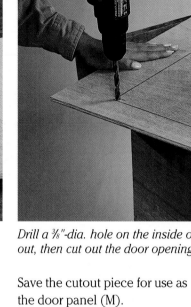

Drill a ⅜"-dia. hole on the inside of one of the corners of the door layout, then cut out the door opening with a jig saw.

posts upright, flush with the ends of the side plates and the the side panels, by driving 2½" deck screws through each plate and into the end of the corresponding post. Drive a 1" deck screw through each side panel and into the corresponding post. Build the second cabinet side panel the same way.

MAKE THE CABINET DOOR FACE FRAME.

1. Cut the face panel (L) to size. On the inside of the panel, mark a cutout for the cabinet door opening. First, measure down from the top 4", and draw a line across the panel. Then, measure in from both sides 2" and draw straight lines across the panel. Finally, draw a line 2" up from the bottom. The layout lines should form an 18½" × 23¼" rectangle.

2. Drill a ⅜"-dia. starter hole for a jig saw blade at one corner of the cutout area **(photo F).** Cut out the door opening with a jig saw. Sand the edges smooth.

Save the cutout piece for use as the door panel (M).

ASSEMBLE THE CABINET.

1. Arrange the cabinet walls so they are 22½" apart. Attach the face frame to a short post on each wall, using glue and 1" deck screws. Make sure the face frame is flush with the outside faces of the cabinet walls, and that the wide "rail" of the face frame is at the top of the cabinet, where there are no plates **(photo G).**

2. Cut the front plate (T) and fasten it to the bottom, inside edge of the face frame, butted against the short posts.

3. Place the cabinet lid assembly onto the cabinet walls and face frame. Attach the cabinet lid with glue. Drive 1" deck screws through the insides of the cabinet walls and into the frame of the lid **(photo H).**

MAKE AND INSTALL THE SHELVES.

1. Cut the shelves (P) to size. Lay out ¾" × 1½" notches in the back corners of the shelves so they fit around the cabinet posts that attach the cabinet to the garage wall. Cut out the notches in the shelves, using a jig saw.

2. On the inside of each cabinet wall, draw lines 8" down from the top and 11" up from the bottom to mark shelf locations. Fit the shelf notches around the back posts, then attach the shelves by driving 1½" deck screws through the cabinet sides and into the edges of the shelves. Drive at least two screws into each shelf edge.

ATTACH THE CABINET TO THE GARAGE.

1. Push the cabinet flush against the left wall of the garage.

2. Fasten the cabinet to the garage by driving 3" deck screws through the garage

Fasten the cutout face frame to the cabinet sides.

Set the cabinet-lid assembly over the cabinet walls and face frame. Fasten them with glue and screws.

Fasten the door rails and door stiles to the door panel using glue and screws, leaving a ¾" overlap on all sides of the door panel.

2. Attach door hinges 3" from the top and bottom of one door stile. Mount the door to the face frame. Install the door pull.

APPLY THE FINISHING TOUCHES.

Sand and smooth the edges of the grill garage and prepare it for the finish of your choice. Since it is constructed with cedar, you can chose a clear wood sealer that leaves the rich wood grain and color visible. If you prefer a painted finish, use a quality primer and durable exterior enamel paint.

posts and into the short posts of the cabinet. Three screws into each post will provide sufficient holding power.

BUILD AND ATTACH THE DOORS.

1. Cut the door rails (N) and stiles (O) to length. Using the cutout from the face frame panel for the door panel (M), fasten the rails and stiles to the door panel using glue and 1½" deck screws. Leave a ¾" overlap on all sides **(photo I)**. Be sure to mount the rails between the stiles, but flush with the stile ends.

TIP
The grill garage is designed as a handy storage center for your grill and such supplies as charcoal and cooking utensils. Do not store heavy items on top of the garage lid, and never light your grill while it is still in the grill garage. Do not store lighter fluid in the grill garage— always keep lighter fluid out of reach of children, in a cool, sheltered area, such as a basement.

Driveway Marker

Build an inviting yard ornament that graces the entrance to your drive-way or front walk and directs foot traffic where you want it to go.

CONSTRUCTION MATERIALS

Quantity	Lumber
1	2 × 4" × 8' cedar
1	1 × 6" × 6' cedar
1	1 × 6" × 8' cedar
4	1 × 2" × 8' cedar

Bestow a sense of order on your front yard by building this handsome cedar driveway marker. Position it on your lawn at the entry to your driveway to keep cars from wandering off the paved surface. Or, set a driveway marker on each side of your front walk to create a formal entry to your home.

This freestanding driveway marker has many benefits you'll appreciate. The fence-style slats slope away from the corner post to create a sense of flow. The broad corner post can be used to mount address numbers, making your home easier to find for visitors and in emergencies. And behind the front slats you'll find a spacious planter.

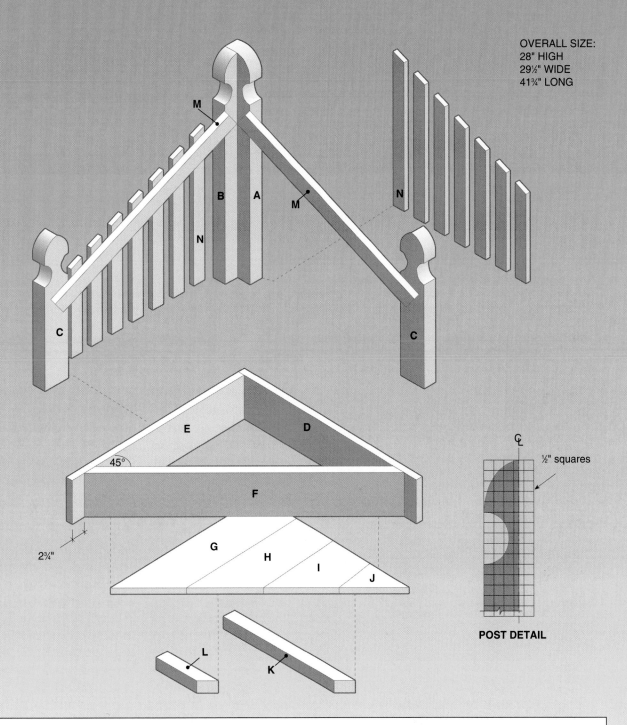

OVERALL SIZE:
28" HIGH
29½" WIDE
41¾" LONG

45°

2¾"

½" squares

POST DETAIL

Key	Part	Dimension	Pcs.	Material
Cutting List				
A	Corner post	1½ × 3½ × 28"	1	Cedar
B	Corner post	1½ × 1½ × 28"	1	Cedar
C	End post	1½ × 3½ × 18½"	2	Cedar
D	Planter side	⅞ × 5½ × 26½"	1	Cedar
E	Planter side	⅞ × 5½ × 25⅝"	1	Cedar
F	Planter back	⅞ × 5½ × 33"	1	Cedar
G	Bottom board	⅞ × 5½ × 23"	1	Cedar

Key	Part	Dimension	Pcs.	Material
Cutting List				
H	Bottom board	⅞ × 5½ × 17"	1	Cedar
I	Bottom board	⅞ × 5½ × 11"	1	Cedar
J	Bottom board	⅞ × 5½ × 6"	1	Cedar
K	Long cleat	1½ × 1½ × 19"	1	Cedar
L	Short cleat	1½ × 1½ × 9"	1	Cedar
M	Stringer	⅞ × 1½ × 27"	2	Cedar
N	Slat	⅞ × 1½ × 20"	14	Cedar

Materials: Moisture-resistant glue, 1¼", 1½", 2" and 2½" deck screws, 2" brass numbers (optional), finishing materials.

Note: Measurements reflect the actual size of dimension lumber.

Rip the thin corner post to width with a circular saw.

Sand the top of the corner post assembly so the joint is smooth.

Lay the bin frame on the bottom boards and trace along the back inside edge to mark cutting lines.

Directions:
Driveway Marker

CUT THE POSTS.

This driveway marker is a free-standing yard ornament supported by single 2 × 4 posts at each end and a doubled 2 × 4 post at the corner.

1. Cut the corner posts (A, B) and end posts (C) to length. Draw a ½"-square grid pattern at the top of one of the end posts, using the grid pattern on page 75 as a reference. Mark a centerpoint at the top of the post and draw the pattern as shown on one side. Reverse the pattern on the other side to create the finished shape. Use a jig saw to cut the end post to shape. Mount a drum sander attachment in your electric drill and use it to smooth out the cut.

2. Use the shaped end post as a template to mark the other end post. Cut and sand it.

3. To make the corner posts, mark centerpoints at the top of each corner post. Trace the contour of one end post on one side of the centerline.

4. On one corner post, draw a line down the length of the post, 2" in from the side with no contour cutout. This will be the narrower post (B). To rip this post to width, attach two pieces of scrap wood to your work surfaces. Screw the post, facedown, to the wood scrap (making sure to drive screws in the waste area of the post).

5. Butt a scrap of the same thickness as the post next to the post, to use as a guide for the circular saw. Attach the guide board to the wood scraps. Set the edge guide on the saw so it follows the outside edge of the scrap. Make the rip cut along the cutting line **(photo A).** Cut the contours at the tops of the corner posts and sand smooth.

BUILD THE CORNER POST.

1. Apply glue to the ripped edge of the narrower post board (B). Lay it on the face of the wider post board (A), so the joint at the corner is flush and the tops of the contours come together in a smooth line.

2. Drill ⅛" pilot holes in the wider board at 4" intervals. Counterbore the holes ¼" deep, using a counterbore bit. Drive 2½" deck screws through the wider board and into the edge of the narrower board. After the glue sets, sand the tops smooth **(photo B).**

MAKE THE
PLANTER FRAME.

The triangular planter fits in the back of the driveway marker.

1. Cut the planter sides (D, E) to length, making square cuts at the ends. The ends of the planter back (F) are mitered so they fit flush against the sides when the bin is formed. Set your circular saw to make a 45° cut. Cut the planter back to length, making sure the bevels

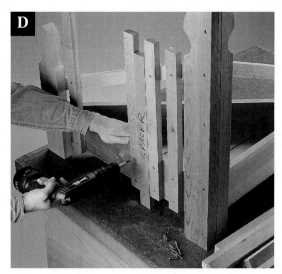

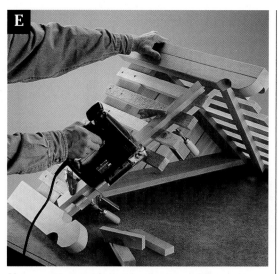

Use one slat as a spacer to set the correct gap as you fasten the slats to the bin and the stringers.

Use a cutting guide to trim the tops of the slats so they extend beyond the tops of the stringers.

both go inward from the same side (see *Diagram,* page 75).

2. Apply glue to the ends of the planter back. Assemble the back and the sides by drilling pilot holes in the outside faces of the sides. Counterbore the holes. Drive 2" deck screws through the sides and into the ends of the back. This will create a setback of about 2¾" from the joints to the ends of the sides.

ATTACH THE BIN BOTTOM.

1. Cut the bottom boards (G, H, I, J) to length. Lay the boards on your work surfaces, arranged from shortest to longest, and butted together edge to edge. Set the bin frame on top of the boards so the inside edges of the frame sides are flush with the outer edges of the boards, and the boards extend past the back edge of the frame. Trace along the inside of the frame back to mark cutting lines on the bottom boards **(photo C).** Cut them with a circular saw.

2. Cut the long cleat (K) and short cleat (L) to length, making a 45° miter cut at one end of each cleat. Turn the planter

bin upside down. Attach the reinforcing cleats so one is 2½"-3" from Side D and the other is about 12" from the same side. Attach them by driving two 2" deck screws through each plant side and back into the end of each cleat.

3. Right the frame. Position the bottom boards flush with the bottom of the frame and attach them with glue and 2" deck screws, driven through the frame and into the ends of the bottom boards.

ATTACH THE BIN AND POSTS.

1. Set the bin on 2"-tall spacers. Fit the corner post assembly over the front corner of the bin and attach with glue and 1½" deck screws.

2. Attach the end posts so each is 29½" away from the corner post assembly.

ATTACH THE STRINGERS AND SLATS.

The stringers (M) are attached between the tops of the posts to support the tops of the slats.

1. Cut the stringers to length. Attach them to the insides of

the posts so the top edges are 1½" below the bottom of the post contour at the point where the stringer meets each post.

2. Cut all slats (N) to length. (The tops will be trimmed after the slats are installed.) Attach them to the bin and the stringers, spaced at 1½" intervals, using 1¼" deck screws. Use a slat as a spacer **(photo D).** Install all 14 slats, making sure the bottoms are flush with the bin bottom.

3. Clamp a piece of 1 × 2 scrap against the outside faces of the slats for a cutting guide—the scrap should be directly opposite the stringer on the back side of the slats. Cut along the guide with a jig saw to trim the slats so the tops are slightly above the top of the stringer **(photo E).**

APPLY FINISHING TOUCHES.

Sand all exposed surfaces and apply two or more coats of exterior wood stain. If your marker will be visible from the curb, you may want to attach 2"-high brass numbers to the corner post to indicate your street address.

Fire Pit Bench

*With seating for three and storage room below,
this versatile bench will be at home anywhere in your yard.*

CONSTRUCTION MATERIALS

Quantity	Lumber
2	2 × 2" × 8' cedar
4	1 × 4" × 8' cedar
4	2 × 4" × 8' cedar
1	1 × 2" × 8' cedar

Summer cookouts, moon-lit bonfires or even a mid-winter warm-up are all perfect occasions to use this cedar fire pit bench. If you are extremely ambitious, you can build four benches to surround your fire pit on all sides. If you don't need that much seating, build only two and arrange them to form a cozy conversation area around the fire. Even without a fire pit, you can build a single bench as a stand-alone furnishing for your favorite spot in the yard or garden.

This solid cedar bench will seat up to three adults comfortably. The slats below give the bench strength, while providing a convenient spot for storing and drying firewood.

OVERALL SIZE:
18" HIGH
18½" WIDE
48" LONG

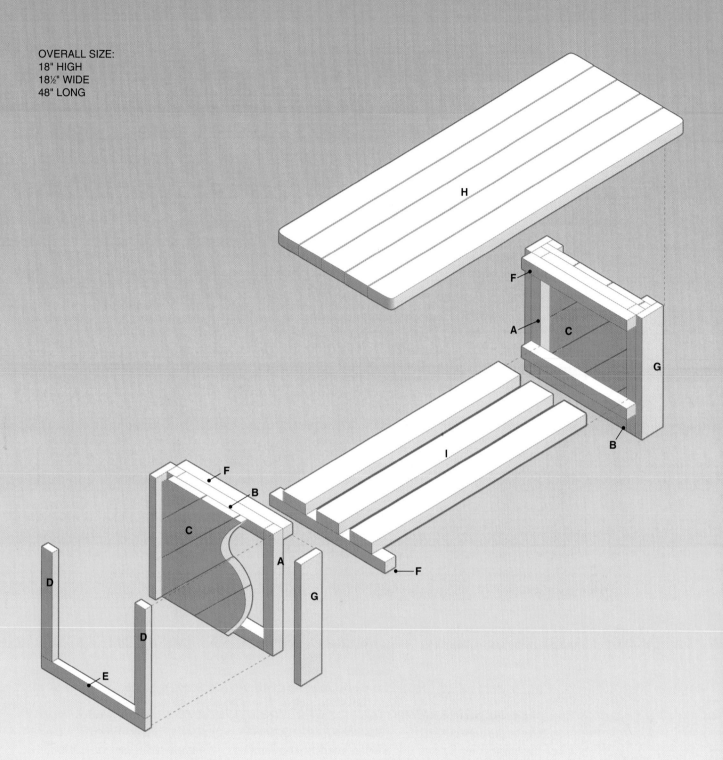

Cutting List

Key	Part	Dimension	Pcs.	Material
A	Frame side	1½ × 1½ × 16½"	4	Cedar
B	Frame end	1½ × 1½ × 14"	4	Cedar
C	End slat	⅞ × 3½ × *	12	Cedar
D	End trim	⅞ × 1½ × 15"	4	Cedar
E	Bottom trim	⅞ × 1½ × 17"	2	Cedar

Cutting List

Key	Part	Dimension	Pcs.	Material
F	Cleat	1½ × 1½ × 17"	4	Cedar
G	Side trim	⅞ × 3½ × 16½"	4	Cedar
H	Seat slat	1½ × 3½ × 48"	5	Cedar
I	Shelf slat	1½ × 3½ × 35"	3	Cedar

Materials: 1½" and 2½" deck screws, finishing materials.

Note: Measurements reflect the actual size of dimension lumber.

* Cut to fit

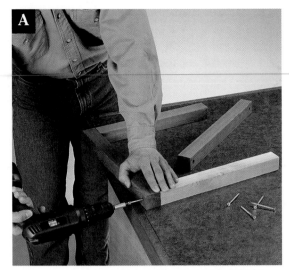

Fasten the frame sides to the frame ends with 2½" galvanized deck screws.

Trim off the ends of the slats so the ends are flush with the outside edges of the end frames.

Directions: Fire Pit Bench

BUILD THE END FRAMES.

1. Cut the frame sides (A) and frame ends (B) to length. Place a frame end between two frame sides. Drill ⅛" pilot holes in the frame sides. Counterbore the holes ¼" deep, using a counterbore bit. Drive 2½" deck screws through the frame sides and into the ends of the frame end **(photo A).** Attach another frame end between the free ends of the frame sides.

2. Follow the same procedure to build the second end frame.

ATTACH THE END SLATS.

The end slats are mounted at 45° angles to the end frames.

1. Lay the frames on a flat surface. Use a combination square as a guide for drawing a reference line at a 45° angle to one corner on each frame, starting 3½" in from the corner.

2. To measure and cut the end slats (C), lay the end of a full-length 1 × 4 cedar board across one frame so one edge meets the corner and the other edge

Use shelf slats to set the correct distance between the end-frame assemblies, then attach the end frames to the bottoms of the seat slats.

follows the reference line. Position the board so the end overhangs the frame by an inch or two. Mark a point with an equal overhang on the other side of the frame.

3. Cut the 1 × 4, then fasten the cut-off piece to the frame by driving pairs of 1½" deck screws into the end frame. Lay a 1 × 4 back across the frame, butted up against the attached

slat, and mark and cut another slat the same way. Attach the slat. Continue cutting and attaching the rest of the slats to cover the frame. Attach slats to the other end frame.

4. Draw straight cutting lines on the tops of the slats, aligned with the outside edges of the end frames. Using a straightedge and circular saw, trim off the ends of the slats along the cutting lines **(photo B).**

Fasten the bottom cleats to the shelf slats, keeping the ends of the slats flush with the outside edges of the cleats.

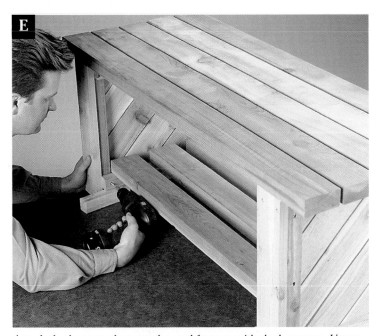

Attach the bottom cleats to the end frames with deck screws. Use a spacer to keep the cleat 1½" up from the bottom of the bench.

COMPLETE THE END FRAMES.

1. Cut the end trim (D) and bottom trim (E) to length. Fasten them to the outside faces of the end slats to create a frame the same length and width as the end frame. Cut the side trim (G) pieces to length and fasten to the frame assembly with 1½" deck screws, making sure the edges of the side trim are flush with the outside edges of the end frames and trim frames.

2. Cut the cleats (F). Fasten a top cleat to the inside of each frame with 2½" deck screws. The top cleats should be flush with the tops of the end frames. (The bottom cleats will be attached later.)

ATTACH THE SEAT SLATS.

1. Cut the seat slats (H) to length. Lay them on a flat surface with the ends flush and ⅛"

spaces between slats. Cut the shelf slats (I). Set the end frame assemblies on top of the seat slats. Slip two of the shelf slats between the ends to set the correct distance.

2. Fasten the end-frame assemblies to the seat slats by driving 1½" deck screws through the cleats on the end frames **(photo C).**

ATTACH THE SHELF SLATS.

1. Arrange the shelf slats on your work surface so the ends are flush, with 1½" gaps between the slats. Lay the remaining two cleats across the ends of the slats. Fasten the cleats to the slats with 2½" deck screws **(photo D).**

2. Set the shelf assembly between the ends of the bench, resting on a 1½" spacer. Attach the shelf by driving 2½" screws through the cleats and into the end frames **(photo E).**

APPLY FINISHING TOUCHES.

1. With a compass, draw a 1½"-radius roundover at the corners of the seat. Cut the roundovers with a jig saw. Sand the entire fire pit bench—especially the edges of the seat slats—to eliminate any possibility of slivers. Or, use a router with a roundover bit to trim off the sharp edges.

2. Apply exterior wood stain to all exposed surfaces.

TIP

When storing firewood, it is tempting to cover the wood with plastic tarps to keep it dry. But more often than not, tarps will only trap moisture and keep the firewood permanently damp. With good ventilation wood dries out quickly, so your best bet is to store it uncovered or in an open shelter.

Plant Boxes

*Build these simple plant boxes in whichever
size or number best meets your needs.*

Quantity	Lumber
3	$1 \times 2" \times 8'$ cedar
6	$1 \times 4" \times 8'$ cedar
1	$\frac{5}{8}" \times 4 \times 8'$ fir siding
1	$\frac{3}{4}" \times 2 \times 4'$ CDX plywood

*To build all three plant boxes as shown

Planters and plant boxes come in a vast array of sizes and styles, and there is a good reason for that. Everyone's needs are different. Rather than build just one planter that may or may not work for you, try this handy planter design. It can easily be changed to fit your space and planting demands.

This project provides measurements for planters in three sizes and shapes: short and broad for flowers or container plants; medium for spices and herbs or small trees and shrubs; and tall and narrow for vegetables or flowering vines that will cascade over the cedar surfaces. The three boxes are proportional to one another— build all three and arrange them in a variety of patterns, including the tiered effect shown above.

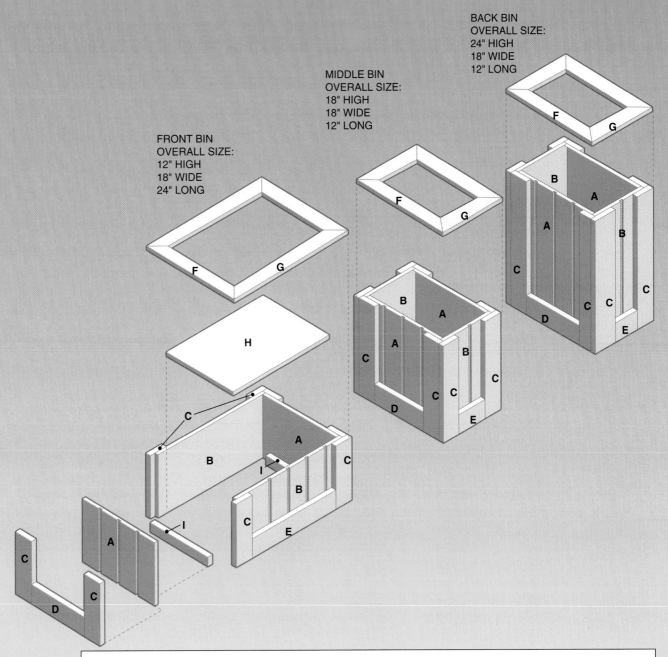

BACK BIN
OVERALL SIZE:
24" HIGH
18" WIDE
12" LONG

MIDDLE BIN
OVERALL SIZE:
18" HIGH
18" WIDE
12" LONG

FRONT BIN
OVERALL SIZE:
12" HIGH
18" WIDE
24" LONG

Cutting List

Key	Part	Front Bin Dimension	Pcs.	Middle Bin Dimension	Pcs.	Back Bin Dimension	Pcs.	Material
A	End panel	⅝ × 15 × 11⅛"	2	⅝ × 15 × 17⅛"	2	⅝ × 15 × 23⅛"	2	Siding
B	Side panel	⅝ × 22¼ × 11⅛"	2	⅝ × 10¼ × 17⅛"	2	⅝ × 10¼ × 23⅛"	2	Siding
C	Corner trim	⅞ × 3½ × 11⅛"	8	⅞ × 3½ × 17⅛"	8	⅞ × 3½ × 23⅛"	8	Cedar
D	Bottom trim	⅞ × 3½ × 9¼"	2	⅞ × 3½ × 9¼"	2	⅞ × 3½ × 9¼"	2	Cedar
E	Bottom trim	⅞ × 3½ × 17"	2	⅞ × 3½ × 5"	2	⅞ × 3½ × 5"	2	Cedar
F	Top cap	⅞ × 1½ × 18"	2	⅞ × 1½ × 18"	2	⅞ × 1½ × 18"	2	Cedar
G	Top cap	⅞ × 1½ × 24"	2	⅞ × 1½ × 12"	2	⅞ × 1½ × 12"	2	Cedar
H	Bottom panel	¾ × 14½ × 19½"	1	¾ × 14½ × 8½"	1	¾ × 14½ × 8½"	1	Plywood
I	Cleat	⅞ × 1½ × 12"	2	⅞ × 1½ × 12"	2	⅞ × 1½ × 12"	2	Cedar

Materials: 1¼", 1½" and 3" deck screws, 6d galvanized finish nails, finishing materials.

Note: Measurements reflect the actual size of dimension lumber.

Directions: Plant Boxes

Whatever the size of the plant box or boxes you are building, you'll use the same basic steps for construction. The only difference between the three boxes is the size of some components. If you need larger, smaller, broader or taller plant boxes than those shown, it's easy to create your own cutting list based on the *Diagram* and dimensions shown on page 83. If you are building several planters, do some planning and sketching to make efficient use of your wood and to save time by gang-cutting parts that are the same size and shape.

MAKE AND ASSEMBLE THE BOX PANELS.

The end and side panels are rectangular pieces of sheet siding fastened together with deck screws. You can use fir sheet siding with 4"-on-center grooves for a decorative look. Or, you can substitute any exterior-rated sheet goods (or even dimension lumber) to match the rest of your yard or home.

1. Cut the end panels (A) and side panels (B) to size, using a circular saw and straightedge cutting guide **(photo A).**

2. Lay an end panel facedown

Cut the end panels and side panels to size using a circular saw and a straightedge cutting guide.

on a flat work surface and butt the side panel, face-side-out, up to the end of the end panel. Mark positions for pilot holes in the side panel. Drill ⅛" pilot holes. Counterbore the holes slightly so the heads are beneath the surface of the wood. Fasten the side panel to the end panel with 1½" deck screws.

3. Position the second side panel at the other end of the end panel and repeat the procedure.

4. Lay the remaining end panel facedown on the work surface. Position the side panel assembly over the end panel, placing the end panel between the side panels and keeping the edges of the side panels flush with the edges of the end panel. Drill pilot holes in the side panels. Counterbore the holes. Fasten the side panels to the end panel with deck screws.

ATTACH THE TRIM.

The cedar trim serves not only as a decorative element, but also as a structural reinforcement to the side panels. Most

cedar has a rough texture on one side. For a rustic look, install your trim pieces with the rough side facing out. For a more finished appearance, install the pieces with the smooth side facing out.

1. Cut the corner trim (C) to length. Overlap the edges of the corner trim pieces at the corners to create a square butt joint. Fasten the corner trim pieces directly to the panels by driving 1¼" deck screws through the inside faces of the panels and into the corner trim pieces **(photo B).** For additional support, drive screws or galvanized finish nails through the overlapping corner trim pieces and into the edges of the adjacent trim piece (this is called "lock-nailing").

2. Cut the bottom trim pieces (D, E) to length. Fasten the pieces to the end and side panels, between the corner trim pieces. Drive 1¼" deck screws through the side and end panels and into the bottom trim pieces.

Fasten the corner trim to the panels by driving deck screws through the panels into the trim.

INSTALL THE TOP CAPS.

The top caps fit around the top of the plant box to create a thin ledge that keeps water from seeping into the end grain of the panels and trim pieces.

1. Cut the top caps (F, G) to length. Cut 45° miters at both ends of one cap piece, using a power miter saw or a miter box and backsaw. Tack the mitered cap piece to the top edge of the planter, keeping the outside edges flush with the outer edges of the corner trim pieces. For a proper fit, use this cap piece as a guide for marking and cutting the miters on the rest of the cap pieces.

2. Miter both ends of each piece and tack it to the box so it makes a square corner with the previously installed piece. If the corners do not work out exactly right, loosen the pieces and adjust the arrangement until everything is square. Permanently fasten all the cap pieces to the box with 6d galvanized finish nails.

INSTALL THE BOX BOTTOM.

The bottom of the planter box is supported by cleats (I) that are fastened inside the box, flush with the bottoms of the side and end panels.

1. Cut the cleats to length. Screw them to the end panels with 1½" deck screws **(photo C).** On the taller bins you may want to mount the cleats higher on the panels so the box won't need as much soil when filled. If you choose to do this, add cleats on the side panels for extra support.

2. Cut the bottom panel (H) to size from ¾"-thick exterior-rated plywood, such as CDX plywood. Set the bottom panel onto the cleats. You do not need to fasten it in place.

APPLY FINISHING TOUCHES.

After you've built all the boxes, sand all the edges and surfaces to remove rough spots and splinters. Apply two or three coats of exterior wood stain to all the surfaces to protect the wood. When the finish has dried, fill the boxes with potting soil. If you are using shorter boxes, you can simply place potted plants inside the planter box.

Attach 1 × 2 cleats to the inside faces of the box ends to support the bottom panel.

Planters

These cedar planters are simple projects that can transform a plain plant container into an attractive outdoor accessory.

CONSTRUCTION MATERIALS

Quantity	Lumber
1	1 × 10" × 6' cedar
1	¼ × 20 × 20" hardboard or plywood

Add a decorative touch to your deck, porch or patio with these stylish cedar planters. Created using square pieces of cedar fashioned together in different design patterns, the styles shown above feature circular cutouts that are sized to hold a standard 24-ounce coffee can. To build them, simply cut 1 × 10 cedar to 9¼" lengths, then make 7¼"-diameter cutouts in the components as necessary. We used a router and template to make the cutouts with production speed. Follow the assembly instructions (see page 89 and the diagrams on page 87) to create the three designs above. Or, you can create your own designs by rearranging the components or altering the cutout size.

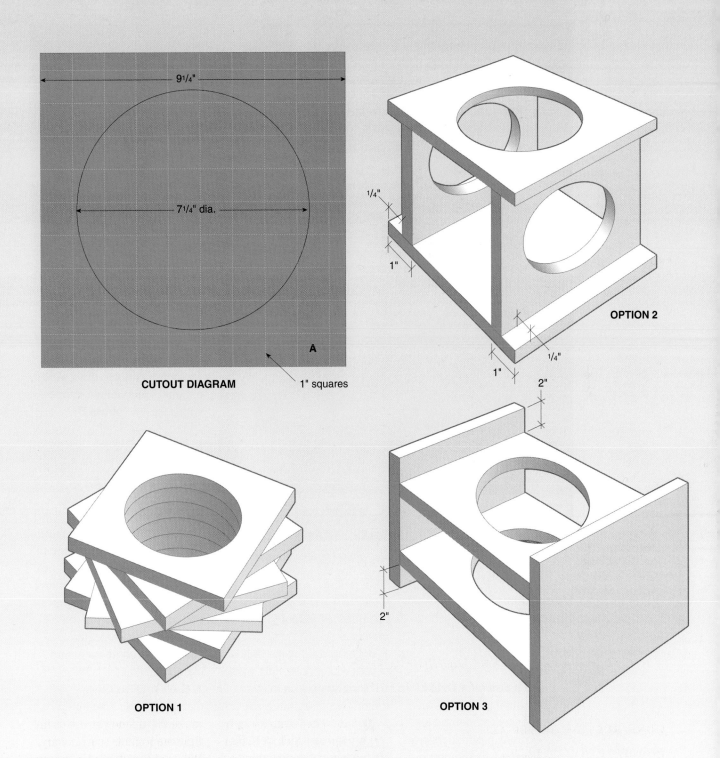

9¼"

7¼" dia.

A

CUTOUT DIAGRAM

1" squares

¼"

1"

OPTION 2

¼"

1"

2"

OPTION 1

2"

OPTION 3

Cutting List				
Key	**Part**	**Dimension**	**Pcs.**	**Material**
A	Component	¾ × 9¼ × 9¼"	*	Cedar

Materials: Moisture-resistant glue, 2" deck screws, 24-ounce coffee can, finishing materials.

* Number of pieces varies according to planter style.

Note: Measurements reflect the actual size of dimension lumber.

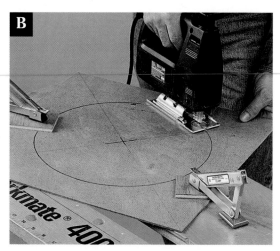

Outline the router base onto scrap material to help determine the router-base radius.

Cut out the router template using a jig saw.

Drill a starter hole for the router bit in the centers of the components.

Add 3⅝" for the radius of a 24-ounce coffee can. Using a compass, draw a circle with this measurement onto the template material. Cut out the template with a jig saw **(photo B).**

MAKE THE PARTS.
The planters are built from identical components (A).
1. Cut the number of components required for your design. Make circular cutouts on those components that require them. To do that, draw diagonal lines connecting the corners of the component. The point of intersection is the center of the square board. Center the template on the component and clamp it in place.
2. Use a drill to bore a 1"-diameter starter hole for the router bit (unless you are using a plunge router—see *Tip,* left) at the center **(photo C).** Position the router bit inside the hole.
3. Turn the router on and move it away from the starter hole until the router base contacts the template. Pull the router in a counterclockwise direction around the inside of the template to make the cutout. Sand sharp edges with sandpaper.

Directions: Planters

MAKE THE ROUTER TEMPLATE.

Using a router and a router template is an excellent method for doing production-style work with uniform results. To create the cutout components for the planters, make a circular template to use as a cutting guide for the router. To determine the size of the template circle, add the radius of your router base to the radius of your finished cutout (3⅝" in the project as shown).
1. Begin by finding the radius of your router base. First, install a 1"-long straight bit in your router. (For fast cutting, use a ¾"-diameter bit, but make sure you use the same bit for making the template and cutting the components.) Make a shallow cut into the edge of a piece of scrap wood. With the router bit stopped, trace around the outside edge of the router base with a pencil **(photo A).**
2. Measure from the perimeter of the router cut to the router-base outline to find the radius.

TIP

Plunge routers are routers with a bit chuck that can be raised or lowered to start internal cuts. If you own a plunge router, use it to cut parts for this project. Otherwise, drill a starter hole as shown, for a standard router.

OPTION 1

Assembly Options

Option 1. *Attach the pieces on the stacked planter from top to bottom, ending with a solid base. To make this stacked planter, you need six pieces of 1 × 10 cedar. Cut them to length, and rout circular shapes in five of them. The solid piece will be the base. Stack the pieces on top of the base component. Place a painted coffee can in the center and arrange the sections to achieve a spiraling effect (see* Diagram, *page 87). Use a pencil to mark the locations of the pieces. Remove the can and fasten the pieces together using glue and deck screws. Attach the pieces by driving the deck screws through the lower pieces into the upper pieces, fastening the base last.*

OPTION 2

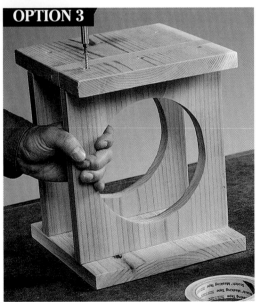

OPTION 3

Option 2. *Use four components on this option to create a planter with three cutout components and a solid base. Measure and mark lines 1" from each side edge on the solid component and one of the cutout components. Attach the inner components with their inside faces flush with these lines. Fasten the solid component to the sides with moisture-resistant glue and deck screws. Attach the remaining cutout component to finish the planter. Insert a painted coffee can.*

Option 3. *Attach two components with circular cutouts to the inside faces of two solid components to make this planter. Measure and mark guidelines 2" from the top and bottom edges on the two solid components. Fasten the two cutout components between the others with moisture-resistant glue and deck screws, making sure their outside edges are flush with the drawn guidelines. Insert a painted coffee can.*

Patio Chair

You won't believe how comfortable plastic tubes can be until you sit in this unique patio chair. It's attractive, reliable and very inexpensive to build.

For solid support, you can't go wrong with this patio chair. Crashing painfully to the ground just when you're trying to sit and relax outdoors is nobody's idea of fun. This patio chair is designed for durability and comfort. It uses rigid plastic tubing for cool, comfortable support that's sure to last through many fun-filled seasons. Say goodbye to expensive or highly-specialized patio furniture with this outdoor workhorse.

This inventive seating project features CPVC plastic tubing that function like slats for the back and seat assemblies. The ½"-dia. tubes have just the right amount of flex and support, and can be purchased at any local hardware store. Even though the tubing is light, there is no danger of this chair blowing away in the wind. It has a heavy, solid frame that will withstand strong gusts of wind and fearsome summer showers. For even greater comfort, you can throw a favorite pillow, pad or blanket over the tubing and arms and relax in the sun.

The materials for this project are inexpensive. All the parts except the seat support are made from 2 × 4 cedar. The seat support is made from 1 × 3 cedar.

CONSTRUCTION MATERIALS

Quantity	Lumber
3	2 × 4" × 10' cedar
1	1 × 3" × 2' cedar
7	½" × 10' CPVC tubing

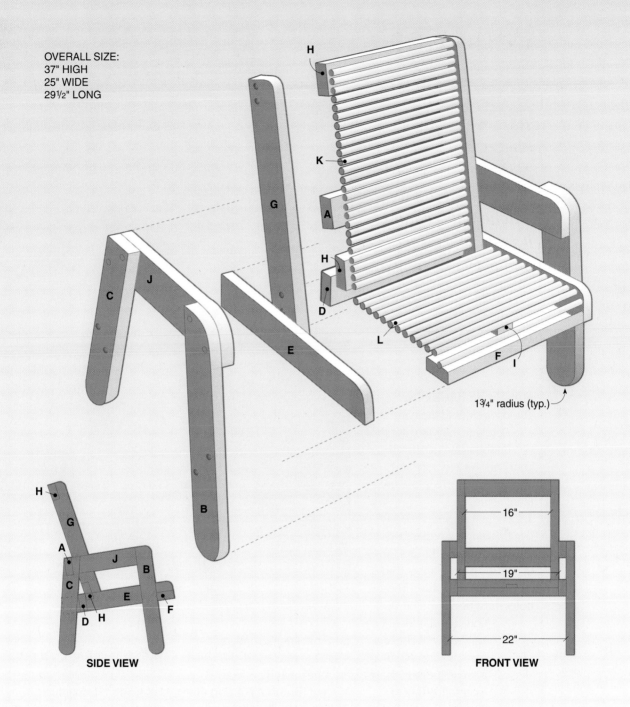

OVERALL SIZE:
37" HIGH
25" WIDE
29½" LONG

1¾" radius (typ.)

SIDE VIEW

FRONT VIEW

16"

19"

22"

Cutting List				
Key	**Part**	**Dimension**	**Pcs.**	**Material**
A	Back support	1½ × 3½ × 19"	1	Cedar
B	Front leg	1½ × 3½ × 22½"	2	Cedar
C	Rear leg	1½ × 3½ × 21"	2	Cedar
D	Seat stop	1½ × 3½ × 19"	1	Cedar
E	Seat side	1½" × 3½ × 24½"	2	Cedar
F	Seat front	1½ × 3½ × 19"	1	Cedar

Cutting List				
Key	**Part**	**Dimension**	**Pcs.**	**Material**
G	Back side	1½ × 3½ × 28"	2	Cedar
H	Back rail	1½ × 3½ × 16"	2	Cedar
I	Seat support	¾ × 2½ × 17¾"	1	Cedar
J	Arm rail	1½ × 3½ × 19½"	2	Cedar
K	Back tube	½-dia. × 17½"	25	CPVC
L	Seat tube	½-dia. × 20½"	14	CPVC

Materials: Moisture-resistant glue, 1¼, 2½ and 3" deck screws, ⅜"-dia. cedar plugs, finishing materials.

Note: Measurements reflect the actual size of dimension lumber.

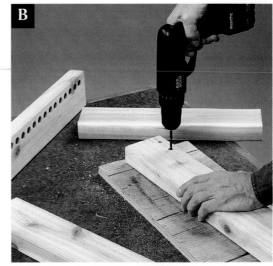

Use a portable drilling guide when drilling the holes for the tubes in the seat sides.

Drill pilot holes before attaching the back rails and sides.

Directions: Patio Chair

MAKE THE BACK SIDES. The back sides of the patio chair provide the frame for the CPVC tubing. Make sure all your cuts are accurate and smooth to achieve good, snug-fitting joints.

1. Cut the back sides (G) to length, using a circular saw.

2. Drill the stopped holes for the plastic tubes on the inside faces of the back sides. These holes must be accurately positioned and drilled. Use a pencil with either a combination square or a straightedge to draw a centering line to mark the locations for the holes. Make the centering line ⅝" from the front edge of each back side.

3. Drill ⅝-dia. × ¾"-deep holes and center them exactly 1" apart along the centerline. Start the first hole 3" from the bottom end of each back side. Use a

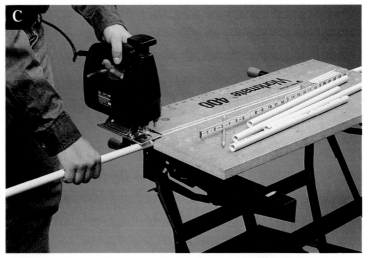

Use a jig saw to cut the CPVC tubing slats. For stability, arrange the tubing so the saw blade is very close to the work surface.

portable drilling guide and a square to make sure the holes are straight and perfectly aligned **(photo A).** A portable drilling guide fits easily onto your power drill to ensure quick and accurate drilling. Some portable drilling guides are equipped with depth stops, making them the next best thing to a standard drill press.

4. Cut 1"-radius roundovers on the top front corner of each back side.

BUILD THE BACK FRAME.

1. Use a circular saw to cut the back rails (H) to length. These pieces will be attached to the inside faces of the back sides.

2. To eliminate the sharp edges, clamp the pieces to a stable work surface and use a sander or a router to soften the edges on the top and bottom of the back rails, and the top edges of the back sides.

3. Dry-fit the back rails and back sides and mark their positions with a pencil.

Attach the remaining side to complete the back assembly.

Attach the seat support to the seat front and seat lock as shown.

4. Drill ⅛" pilot holes in the back side and counterbore the holes to a ¼" depth, using a counterbore bit. **(photo B).**
5. Apply moisture-resistant glue to one end of each rail and fasten the rails to a single back side with 3" deck screws.

COMPLETE THE BACK ASSEMBLY.

Before assembling the back, you need to prepare the CPVC tubing for the frame holes. Make sure the tubing is ½"-dia. CPVC, which is rated for hot water. This plastic tubing is usually available in 10' lengths. (Standard PVC tubing is not usually sold in small diameters

that will fit the ⅝"-dia. holes you have drilled.)
1. Use a jig saw to cut 25 pieces of the ½"-dia. CPVC tubing. Remember, these pieces will be used for the back seat assembly only. The seat assembly requires additional pieces. Cut the back tubes to 17½" lengths **(photo C).**
2. Wash the grade stamps off the tubing with lacquer thinner. (Wear gloves and work in a well-ventilated area when using lacquer thinner.) Rinse the tubing with clean water.
3. Once the pipes are clean and dry, insert them into the holes on one of the back sides. Slide the remaining back side into place, positioning the plastic tubes into the holes.
4. Attach the rails to the back side by driving 3" deck screws through the pilot holes **(photo D).**

BUILD THE SEAT FRAME.

One important difference between the seat frame and the back frame is the positioning of the CPVC tubing. On the seat frame, one tube is inserted into the sides slightly out of line at the front to make the chair more comfortable for your legs.
1. Cut the seat sides (E), seat front (F), seat stop (D) and seat support (I) to length. Use the

TIP

The easiest way to cut CPVC tubing is with a power miter box, but no matter what kind of saw you are using, remember to work in a well-ventilated room. Although plastic tubing generally cuts easily without melting or burning, it can release some toxic fumes as it is cut. When you're finished, you might consider treating the tubes with some automotive plastic polish to help preserve them.

same methods as with the back frame to draw the centering line for the plastic tubing on the seat sides. Drill the tube holes into each seat side. Start the holes 2" from the front end of the seat sides.

2. Position a single tube hole on the seat frame ⅞" below the top edge and 1" from the front end of each seat side. This front tube provides a gradual downward seat profile for increased leg comfort.

3. To eliminate the sharp edges on the seat assembly, round the seat sides, seat support edges and seat front edges with a sander or router. Cut 1"-radius roundovers on the top front corners of the seat sides.

4. Use a combination square to mark a line across the width of the inside of the seat sides, 3½" from the back edges. This is where the back face of the seat stop is positioned. Test-fit the pieces to make sure their positions are correct. Lay out and mark the position of the seat stop and seat front on each seat side.

5. Drill pilot holes to fasten one of the seat sides to the seat stop and seat front, as you did with the back assembly. Counterbore the holes. Connect the parts with moisture-resistant glue and deck screws.

Make identical radius cuts on the bottoms of the legs.

Use a square to make sure the seat is perpendicular to the leg.

COMPLETE THE SEAT FRAME.

1. Cut 14 pieces of ½"-dia. CPVC pipe. Each piece should be 20½" long. Once again, clean the grade stamps off the tubes with lacquer thinner and rinse them with clean water. Let them dry and insert them into the holes on one seat side.

2. Carefully slide the remaining seat side into place and fasten the pieces with moisture resistant glue and deck screws.

3. Position the seat support (I) under the tubing in the center of the seat. Attach the seat support to the middle of the seat front and seat stop with moisture-resistant glue and 1¼" deck screws **(photo E).**

BUILD THE ARMS AND LEGS.

The arms and legs are all that remain for the patio chair assembly. When you make the radius cuts on the bottom edges of the front and back legs, make sure the cuts are exactly the same on each leg (see *Diagram,* page 91). Otherwise, the legs may be uneven and rock back and forth when you sit.

Slide the back frame into the seat frame so the back sides rest against the seat stop and seat support.

1. Cut the back support (A), front legs (B), rear legs (C) and arm rails (J) to length.
2. Use a jig saw to cut a full-radius roundover on the bottoms of the legs **(photo F).** Cut a 1"-radius roundover on the top front corners of the arms and the front legs.
3. To attach the front legs to the outsides of the arm rails, drill pilot holes in the front legs and counterbore the holes. Then, attach the parts at a 90° angle, using 2½" deck screws. The legs should be flush with the front ends of the rails.
4. Attach the leg/arm rail assembly to the seat frame so that the top edge of the seat frame is 15" from the bottom of the leg. The front of the seat should

extend exactly 3½" past the leg. Use a square to make sure the seat is perpendicular to the legs **(photo G).**
5. To attach the rear legs, drill pilot holes in the rear legs and counterbore the holes. Attach the rear legs to the arm rails and seat sides with glue. Then, drive 2½" deck screws through the rear legs and into the arm rails and seat sides. The back edge of the legs should be flush with the ends of the arm rails and seat sides. Trim the excess material from the tops of the legs so they are flush with the tops of the arm rails.
6. To attach the back support, drill pilot holes in the arm rails. Counterbore the holes. Then, attach the back support be-

tween the rails with glue and drive 2½" deck screws through the arm rails and into the back support. The back support should be flush with the ends of the arm rails.
7. Round and sand all rough edges smooth.

ATTACH THE BACK FRAME.
1. Slide the back frame into the seat frame **(photo H)** so that the back sides rest against the seat stop and the back rail rests on the seat support.
2. Drill pilot holes in the seat stop and counterbore the holes. Apply glue, and attach the back frame by driving deck screws through the seat stop and into the back rail.

APPLY FINISHING TOUCHES.
1. For a refined look, apply glue to the bottoms of ⅜"-dia. cedar wood plugs, and insert the plugs into the screw counterbores. Sand the tops of the plugs until they are flush with the surrounding surface.
2. Wipe the chair with mineral spirits and finish the chair with a clear wood sealer.

TIP

When using a jig saw, it is tempting to speed up a cut by pushing the tool with too much force. When cutting curves or roundovers, this is likely to cause the saw blade to bend. This often causes irregular cuts and burns, especially when working with cedar. You can achieve smoother curves and roundovers with multiple gentle passes with the saw, until the proper curve is achieved. Finish the job by sanding the curves smooth.

Firewood Shelter

*Those stacks of firewood won't be an eyesore anymore once you
build this ranch-style firewood shelter for your yard.*

CONSTRUCTION MATERIALS

Quantity	Lumber
10	2 × 4" × 8' cedar
5	2 × 6" × 8' cedar
10	⅝ × 8" × 8' cedar lap siding

This handsome firewood shelter combines rustic ranch styling with ample sheltered storage that keeps firewood off the ground and obscured from sight. Clad on the sides and roof with beveled cedar lap siding, the shelter has the look and feel of a permanent structure. But because it's freestanding, you can move it around as needed. It requires no time-consuming foundation work.

This firewood shelter is large enough to hold an entire face cord of firewood. And since the storage area is sheltered and raised to avoid ground contact and allow air flow, wood dries quickly and is ready to use when you need it.

OVERALL SIZE:
62" HIGH
32" DEEP
8' LONG

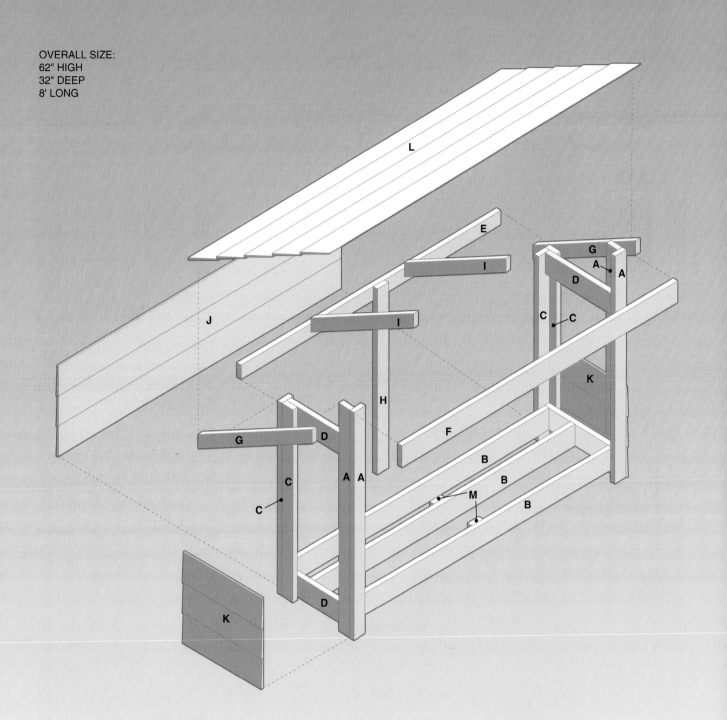

Cutting List

Key	Part	Dimension	Pcs.	Material	Key	Part	Dimension	Pcs.	Material
A	Front post	1½ × 3½ × 59"	4	Cedar	**H**	Middle post	1½ × 3½ × 50"	1	Cedar
B	Bottom rail	1½ × 5½ × 82½"	3	Cedar	**I**	Middle support	1½ × 3½ × 28"	2	Cedar
C	Rear post	1½ × 3½ × 50"	4	Cedar	**J**	Back siding	⅝ × 8 × 88½"	3	Cedar siding
D	End rail	1½ × 5½ × 21"	4	Cedar	**K**	End siding	⅝ × 8 × 24"	6	Cedar siding
E	Back rail	1½ × 3½ × 88½"	1	Cedar	**L**	Roof strip	⅝ × 8 × 96"	5	Cedar siding
F	Front rail	1½ × 5½ × 88½"	1	Cedar	**M**	Prop	1½ × 3½ × 7½"	2	Cedar
G	Roof support	1½ × 3½ × 33¾"	2	Cedar					

Materials: ⅜ × 3½" lag screws (24), ⅜ × 4" lag screws (8), 1½" spiral siding nails, 2½" and 3" deck screws, finishing materials.

Note: Measurements reflect the actual size of dimension lumber.

Directions:
Firewood Shelter

BUILD THE FRAME.

1. Cut the front posts (A) and rear posts (C) to length. Butt the edges of the front posts together in pairs to form the corner posts. Drill ⅛" pilot holes at 8" intervals. Counterbore the holes ¼" deep, using a counterbore bit. Join the post pairs with 2½" deck screws. Follow the same procedure to join the rear posts in pairs.
2. Cut the bottom rails (B) and end rails (D). Assemble two bottom rails and two end rails into a rectangular frame, with the end rails covering the ends of the bottom rails. Set the third bottom rail between the end rails, centered between the other bottom rails. Mark the ends of the bottom rails on the outside faces of the end rails. Drill two ⅜" pilot holes for lag screws through the end rails at each bottom rail position—do not drill into the bottom rails. Drill a ¾" counterbore for each pilot hole, deep enough to recess the screw heads. Drill a smaller, ¼" pilot hole through each pilot hole in the end rails, into the ends of the bottom rails **(photo A).** Drive a ⅜ × 3½" lag screw fitted with a washer at each pilot hole, using a socket wrench.
3. Draw reference lines across the inside faces of the corner posts, 2" up from the bottoms. With the corner posts upright and about 82" apart, set 2"-high spacers next to each corner post to support the frame. Position the bottom rail frame between the corner posts, and attach the frame to the corner posts by driving two 2½" deck screws through the corner posts and into the outer faces of the bottom rails. Drill pilot holes in the sides of the corner posts. Counterbore the holes. Drive a pair of ⅜ × 4" lag screws, fitted with washers, through the sides of the corner posts and into the bottom rails. The lag screws must go through the post and end rail, and into the end of the bottom rail. Avoid hitting the lag screws that have already been driven through the end rails.
4. Complete the frame by installing end rails at the tops of the corner posts. Drill pilot holes in the end rails. Counterbore the holes. Drive 2½" deck screws through the end rails and into the posts. Make sure the tops of the end rails are flush with the tops of the rear posts **(photo B).**

MAKE THE ROOF FRAME.

1. Cut the back rail (E), front rail (F), roof supports (G), middle post (H) and middle supports (I) to length. The roof supports and middle supports are mitered at the ends. To make the miter cutting lines, mark a point 1½" in from each end, along the edge of the board. Draw diagonal lines from each point to the opposing corner. Cut along the lines

Use a smaller bit to extend the pilot holes for the lag screws into the ends of the bottom rails.

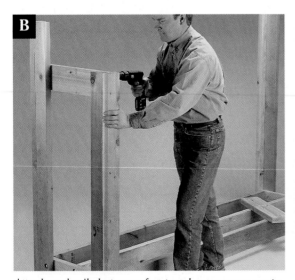

Attach end rails between front and rear corner posts.

Miter-cut the middle supports and roof supports with a circular saw.

Attach the front rail by driving screws through the outer roof supports, making sure the top of the rail is flush with the tops of the supports.

Attach the middle roof supports by driving screws through the front and back rails.

with a circular saw **(photo C).**

2. Drill pilot holes in the back rail. Counterbore the holes. Use 3" deck screws to fasten the back rail to the backs of the rear corner posts, flush with their tops and sides. Use the same procedure to fasten a roof support to the outsides of the corner posts. Make sure the top of each support is flush with the high point of each post end. The supports should overhang the posts equally in the front and rear.

3. Drill pilot holes in the roof supports. Counterbore the holes. Drive deck screws to attach the front rail between the roof supports **(photo D),** with the top flush with the tops of the roof supports. Attach the middle supports between the front rail and back rail, 30" in from each rail end. Drive 3" deck screws through the front and back rails into the ends of the middle supports **(photo E).** Use a pipe clamp to hold the supports in place as you attach them.

4. Drill pilot holes in the middle post (H). Counterbore the holes. Position the middle post

so it fits against the outside of the rear bottom rail and the inside of the top back rail. Make sure the middle post is perpendicular and extends past the bottom rail by 2". Attach it with 2½" deck screws.

5. Cut a pair of props (M) to length. Attach them to the front two bottom rails, aligned with the middle post. Make sure the tops of the props are flush with the tops of the bottom rails.

ATTACH SIDING AND ROOF.

1. Cut pieces of 8"-wide beveled cedar lap siding to length to make the siding strips (J, K) and the roof strips (L). Starting 2" up from the bottoms of the rear posts, fasten the back siding strips (J) with two 1½" siding nails driven through each strip and into the posts, near the top and bottom edge of the strip. Work your way up, overlapping each piece of siding by ½", making sure the thicker edges of the siding face down. Attach the end siding (K) to the corner posts, with the seams aligned with the seams in the back siding.

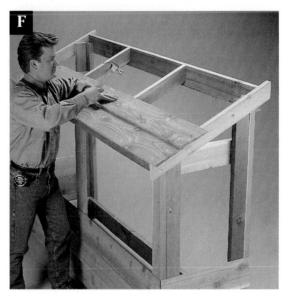

Attach the roof strips with siding nails, starting at the back edge and working your way forward.

2. Attach the roof strips (L) to the roof supports, starting at the back edge. Drive two nails into each roof support. Make sure the wide edge of the siding faces down. Attach the rest of the roof strips, overlapping the strip below by about ½" **(photo F),** until you reach the front edges of the roof supports. You can leave the cedar wood untreated or apply an exterior wood stain to keep it from turning gray as it weathers.

Sun Lounger

Designed for the dedicated sun worshipper, this sun lounger has a backrest that can be set in either a flat or an upright position.

CONSTRUCTION MATERIALS

Quantity	Lumber
3	2 × 2" × 8' pine
1	2 × 4" × 8' pine
5	2 × 4" × 10' pine
2	2 × 6" × 10' pine

Leave your thin beach towel and flimsy plastic chaise lounge behind, as you relax and soak up the sun in this solid wood sun lounger. Set the adjustable backrest in an upright position while you make your way through your summer reading list. Then, for a change of pace, set the backrest in the flat position and drift off in a pleasant reverie. If you're an ambitious suntanner, take comfort in the fact that this sun lounger is lightweight enough that it can be moved easily to follow the path of direct sunlight. Made almost entirely from inexpensive pine or cedar, this sun lounger can be built for only a few dollars—plus a little sweat equity.

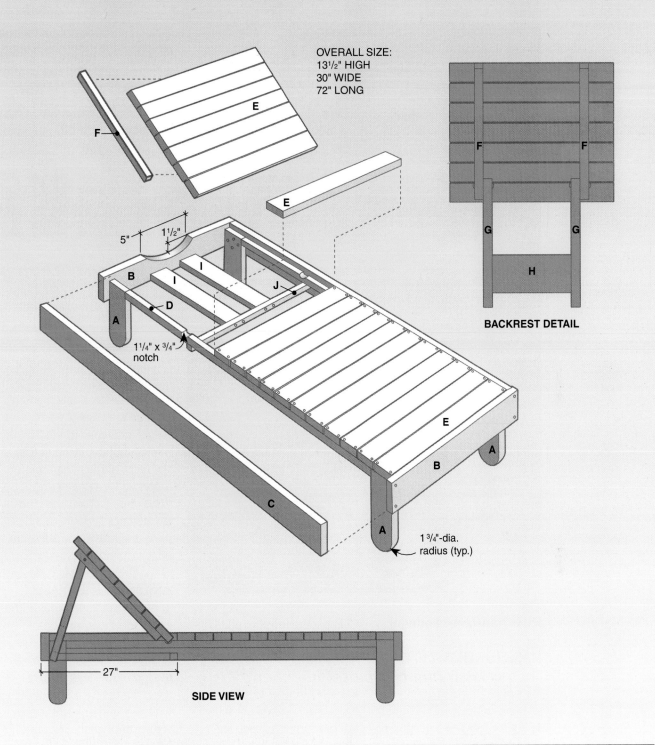

OVERALL SIZE:
13½" HIGH
30" WIDE
72" LONG

F

E

E

5" 1½"

B

I I

A D

1¼" × ¾" notch

J

C

A

E

B

A

1¾"-dia. radius (typ.)

BACKREST DETAIL

F F

G G

H

27"

SIDE VIEW

Cutting List				
Key	**Part**	**Dimension**	**Pcs.**	**Material**
A	Leg	1½ × 3½ × 12"	4	Pine
B	Frame end	1½ × 5½ × 30"	2	Pine
C	Frame side	1½ × 5½ × 69"	2	Pine
D	Ledger	1½ × 1½ × 62"	2	Pine
E	Slat	1½ × 3½ × 27"	19	Pine

Cutting List				
Key	**Part**	**Dimension**	**Pcs.**	**Material**
F	Back brace	1½ × 1½ × 22"	2	Pine
G	Back support	1½ × 1½ × 20"	2	Pine
H	Cross brace	1½ × 5½ × 13"	1	Pine
I	Slide support	1½ × 3½ × 24"	2	Pine
J	Slide brace	1½ × 1½ × 27"	1	Pine

Materials: Moisture-resistant wood glue, 2½" deck screws, ¼"-dia. × 3½" carriage bolts (2) with washers and nuts.

Note: Measurements reflect the actual size of dimension lumber.

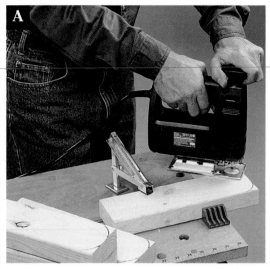

Use a jig saw to cut roundovers on the bottoms of the legs.

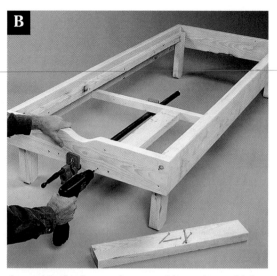

Assemble the frame pieces and legs, then add the support boards for the slats and backrest.

Use ⅛"-thick spacers to keep an even gap between slats as you fasten them to the back braces and the ledgers in the bed frame.

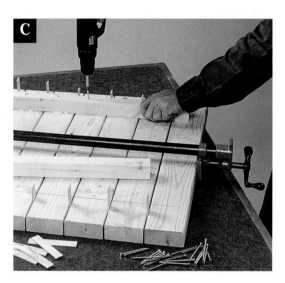

Directions: Sun Lounger

MAKE THE LEGS.
The rounded leg bottoms help the sun lounger rest firmly on uneven surfaces.
1. Cut the legs (A) to length. To ensure uniform length, cut four 2 × 4s to about 13" in length.

Clamp them together edge to edge and gang-cut them to final length (12") with a circular saw.
2. Use a compass to scribe a 3½"-radius roundoff cut at the bottom corners of each leg. Make the roundoff cuts with a jig saw **(photo A).** Sand smooth.

CUT THE FRAME PIECES AND LEDGERS.
1. Cut the frame ends (B) and frame sides (C) to length. Use a jig saw to cut a 5"-wide, 1½"-deep notch into the top edge of one frame end, centered end to end, to create a handgrip.

2. Cut the ledgers (D) to length. Measure 24" from one end of each ledger. Place a mark, then cut a 1¼"-wide, ¾"-deep notch into the top edge of each ledger, centered on the 24" mark. Smooth out the notch with a 1½"-radius drum sander mounted on a power drill. (This mark will serve as a pivot for the back support.) Sand all parts and smooth out all sharp edges.

ASSEMBLE THE FRAME.
1. Attach the frame sides and frame ends to form a box around the legs, with the tops of the frame pieces 1½" above the tops of the legs to leave space for the 2 × 4 slats. Fasten with glue and drive 2½" deck screws through the legs and into the frame sides. Also drive screws through the frame ends and into the legs.
2. Attach the ledgers to the frame sides, fitted between the legs, using glue and 2½" deck screws. Make sure the ledger tops are flush with the tops of the legs and the notches are at the same end as the notch in the frame.

TIP

For a better appearance, always keep the screws aligned. In some cases, you may want to add some screws for purely decorative purposes: in this project, we drove 1" deck screws into the backrest slats to continue the lines created by the screw heads in the lower lounge slats.

CUT AND INSTALL THE BACKREST SUPPORTS.

1. Cut the slide brace (J) to length. Position the slide brace between the frame sides, 24" from the notched frame end, fitted against the bottom edges of the ledgers. Glue and screw the slide brace to the bottom edges of the ledgers.

2. Cut the slide supports (I) to length. Position the supports so they are about 3" apart, centered below the notch in the frame end. The ends of the supports should fit neatly against the frame end and the slide brace. Attach with glue and drive screws through the frame end and the slide brace, and into the ends of the slide supports **(photo B).**

FASTEN THE SLATS.

1. Cut all the slats (E) to length. Use a straightedge guide to ensure straight cuts (the ends will be highly visible). Or, simply hold a speed square against the edges of the boards and run your circular saw along the edge of the speed square.

2. Cut the back braces (F) to length. Lay seven of the slats on a flat work surface, and slip ⅛"-wide spacers between the slats. With the ends of the slats flush, set the back braces onto the faces of the slats, 4" in from the ends. Drive a 2½" deck screw through the brace and into each slat **(photo C).**

3. Install the remaining slats in the lounge frame, spaced ⅛" apart, by driving two screws through each slat end and into the tops of the ledgers. One end slat should be ⅛" from the inside of the uncut frame end, and the other 27" from the outside of the notched frame end.

ASSEMBLE THE BACKREST SUPPORT FRAMEWORK.

The adjustable backrest is held in place by a small framework attached to the back braces. The framework can either be laid flat so the backrest lies flat, or raised up and fitted against the inside of the notched frame end to support the upright backrest.

1. Cut the back supports (G) to length. Clamp the pieces together face to face, with the ends flush. Clamp a belt sander to your work surface, and use it as a grinder to round off the supports on one end.

2. Cut the cross brace (H) to length. Position the cross brace between the back supports, 2" from the non-rounded ends. Attach with glue and drive 2½" deck screws through the supports and into the cross brace.

3. Position the rounded ends of the supports so they fit between the ends of the back braces, overlapping by 2½" when laid flat. Drill a ¼" guide hole through the braces and the supports at each overlap joint.

4. Thread ¼"-dia. × 3½"-long carriage bolts through the guide holes, with a flat washer between each support and brace. Hand-tighten a washer and nylon locking nut onto each bolt end (see **photo D).**

INSTALL THE BACKREST.

1. Set the backrest onto the ledger boards near the notched end of the frame.

2. With the backrest raised, tighten the locking nut on the backrest support framework until it holds the framework together securely while still allowing the joint to pivot **(photo D).**

APPLY FINISHING TOUCHES.

Sand all surfaces and edges **(photo E)** to eliminate slivers. Apply two coats of water-based, exterior polyurethane for a smooth, protective finish. Or, use a primer and a light-colored exterior paint.

Use a washer and nylon locking nut to fasten the back braces to the back supports.

Sand all surfaces carefully to eliminate splinters, and check to make sure all screw heads are set below the wood surface.

Fold-up Lawn Seat

*With this fold-up seat built for two, you won't have to
sacrifice comfort and style for portability.*

CONSTRUCTION MATERIALS

Quantity	Lumber
1	2 × 8" × 6' cedar
4	2 × 4" × 8' cedar
2	1 × 6" × 8' cedar

E ven though this cedar lawn seat folds up for easy transport and storage, it is sturdier and more attractive than just about any outdoor seating you are likely to make or buy. The backrest and legs lock into place when the seat is in use. To move or store this two-person seat, simply fold the backrest down and tuck the legs into the seat frame to convert the seat into a compact package.

Because it is portable and stores in a small space, you can keep the fold-up lawn seat tucked away in a garage or basement and set it up for extra seating when you are entertaining. Or, if security around your home is an issue, you can bring it inside easily during times when you're not home.

OVERALL SIZE:
34⅛" HIGH
22" DEEP
42" LONG

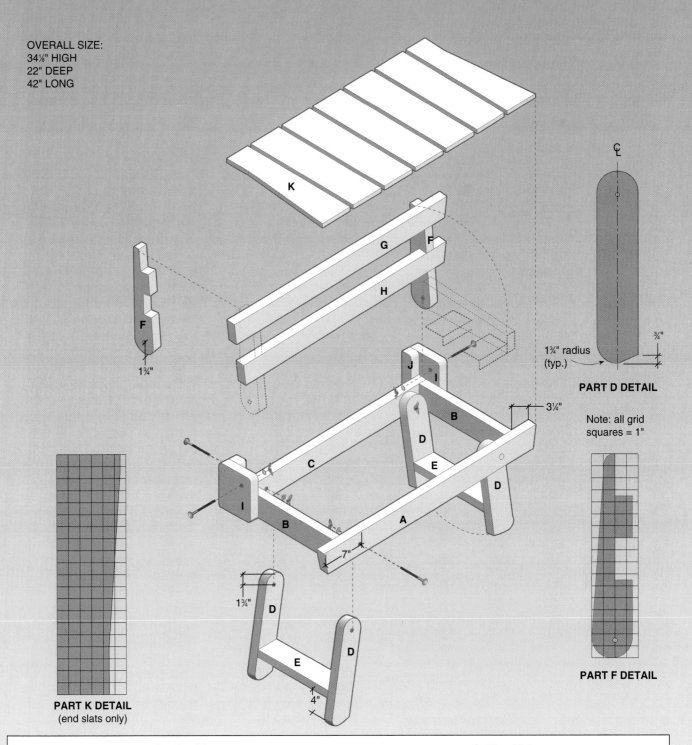

PART D DETAIL

1¾" radius
(typ.)

¾"

Note: all grid
squares = 1"

3¼"

7"

1¾"

4"

PART F DETAIL

PART K DETAIL
(end slats only)

Key	Part	Dimension	Pcs.	Material
A	Front seat rail	1½ × 3½ × 42"	1	Cedar
B	Side seat rail	1½ × 3½ × 17"	2	Cedar
C	Back seat rail	1½ × 3½ × 35½"	1	Cedar
D	Leg	1½ × 3½ × 16¼"	4	Cedar
E	Stretcher	1½ × 3½ × 13⅞"	2	Cedar
F	Backrest post	1½ × 3½ × 17"	2	Cedar

Cutting List

Key	Part	Dimension	Pcs.	Material
G	Top rest	1½ × 3½ × 42"	1	Cedar
H	Bottom rest	1½ × 3½ × 40"	1	Cedar
I	Cleat	1½ × 7¼ × 6"	2	Cedar
J	Stop	1½ × 7¼ × 2"	2	Cedar
K	Slat	⅞ × 5½ × 20"	7	Cedar

Cutting List

Materials: Moisture-resistant glue, ⅜ × 4" carriage bolts (6) with washers and wing nuts, 1¼", 2" and 2½" deck screws.

Note: Measurements reflect the actual size of dimension lumber.

Directions:
Fold-up Lawn Seat

MAKE THE LEGS.

The lawn seat is supported by two H-shaped legs that fold up inside the seat.

1. Cut the legs (D) to length. Mark a point 1¾" in from one end of each leg. Make sure the point is centered on the leg.

2. Set the point of a compass on each point and draw a 1¾"-radius semicircle to make a cutting line for a roundover at the top of each leg. Cut the roundovers with a jig saw. Then, drill a ⅜"-dia. pilot hole through each point.

3. At the other end of each leg, mark a centerpoint measured from side to side. Measure in ¾" from the end along one edge, and mark another point. Connect the points with a

Fasten the stretchers between the legs with glue and deck screws.

Smooth out the post notches with a wood file.

straight line, and cut along the line with a jig saw to create the flat leg bottoms.

4. Mark 1¾"-radius roundovers at the opposite edges of the leg bottoms, using the approach from Steps 1 and 2. Cut the roundovers with a jig saw.

5. Measure 5½" from the flat end of each leg and drill two pilot holes, 1" from the edge. Counterbore the holes to ¼" depth, using a counterbore bit.

6. Cut the stretchers (E) to length. Attach one stretcher between each pair of legs so the bottoms of the stretchers are 4" from the bottoms of the legs **(photo A)**. Attach the legs with glue and drive 2½" deck screws through the pilot holes. Check that the flat ends of the legs are at the same end.

MAKE THE BACKREST POSTS.

Two posts are notched to hold the two boards that form the backrest.

1. Cut the backrest posts (F) to size. On one edge of each post, mark points 6½", 10" and 13½" from the end of the post. Draw a line lengthwise on each post, 1½" in from the edge with the marks. Extend lines from each point across the lengthwise line. These are the outlines for the notches in the posts (see *Diagram*, page 105). Use a jig saw to cut the notches, then file or sand the cuts smooth **(photo B)**.

2. Use a compass to draw a semicircle with a 1¾" radius at the bottom of each post. Measure 1¾" from the bottoms, and mark drilling points centered side to side. Drill a ⅜"-dia. pilot hole at each point.

3. Mark 1" tapers on the back edges of the posts (see *Part F Detail*, page 105). Cut the tapers with a jig saw. Then, sand the posts smooth. Make sure to sand away any sharp edges.

ASSEMBLE THE BACKREST.

1. Cut the top rest (G) and bottom rest (H). Mark trim lines at the ends, starting ½" in from the ends on one edge and tapering to the opposite corner. Check that the trim lines on each end are symmetrical. Trim the ends with a jig saw.

2. Position the posts on their back (tapered) edges, and insert the top and bottom rests into their notches. Position the posts 32½" apart. Center the rests on the posts. The overhang should be equal on each rest. Then, attach the rests to the posts with glue and 2" deck screws **(photo C)**.

BUILD THE SEAT FRAME.

The seat frame is made by attaching two side rails between a front rail and back rail. The front rail is tapered to match the backrest.

1. Cut the front seat rail (A), side seat rails (B) and back seat rail (C) to length. Sand the parts smooth.

2. Drill three evenly spaced ⅛" pilot holes, 4" in from each end of the front rail to attach the side rails. Counterbore the holes, using a ¼" drill bit. Make a ½" taper cut at each end of the front rail.

3. Drill centered, ⅜"-dia. holes, 7" in from each end for the leg assemblies. Also drill ⅜"-dia. pilot holes for carriage bolts through the back rail, centered 3¾" in from each end.

4. Apply moisture-resistant glue to one end of each side rail, and position the side rails against the front rails. Fasten the side rails to the back of the front rail by driving deck screws through the pilot holes in the front rail and into the ends of the side rails.

5. Fasten the back rail to the free ends of the side rails with glue and screws. Check that the ends are flush. Then, sand

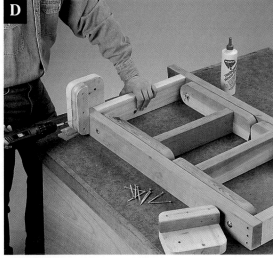

Center the top and bottom rests in the post notches, and fasten them with glue and deck screws.

Attach the cleats and stops to the rear edges of the seat frame.

Attach the backrest to the seat frame with carriage bolts and wing nuts.

the frame to round the bottom outside edges.

JOIN THE LEGS AND SEAT FRAME.

1. Position the leg assemblies inside the seat frame. Make certain the rounded corners face the ends of the frame.
2. Apply paste wax to four carriage bolts. Align the pilot holes in the legs and seat frame, and attach the parts with the carriage bolts (see *Diagram*, page 105).

ATTACH THE CLEATS AND STOP.

The cleats (I) and stops (J) are attached to each other on the back corner of the seat frame to provide an anchor for the backrest. Once the cleats and stops are attached, carriage bolts are driven through the cleats and into the posts on the backrest. The stops fit flush with the back edges of the cleats to prevent the backrest from folding all the way over.
1. Cut the cleats and stops to size. Then, position a stop against a cleat face, flush with one long edge. The top and bottom edges must be flush. Attach the stop to the cleat with glue and 2½" deck screws.

2. Drill a ⅜"-dia. hole through each cleat, centered 1¾" in from the front and top edges.
3. Smooth the edges of the cleats and stops with a sander. Attach them to the rear corners of the seat frame with glue and 2½" deck screws **(photo D).** Make certain the bottom edges of the cleats and stops are ½" above the bottom of the frame.

ATTACH THE SEAT SLATS.

The seat slats are all the same length, but the end slats are tapered from front to back.
1. Cut the slats (K). Then, plot a 1"-grid on two of the slats (see *Part K Detail*, page 105).
2. Draw cutting lines at the edges of the two slats (see *Part K Detail*). NOTE: the taper straightens 4" from the back of the slat). Cut the tapers with a circular saw or jig saw. Smooth the edges with a router and roundover bit, or a sander.
3. Attach the slats to the seat frame, using glue and 1¼" screws. Make sure the wide ends of the end slats are flush with the ends of the frame, and the back ends of all slats are flush with the back edge of the frame. The gaps between slats should be equal.

ASSEMBLE THE LAWN SEAT.

1. Finish all of the parts with an exterior wood stain.
2. Fit the backrest assembly between the cleats. Align the holes in the posts and cleats, and insert the bolts.
3. Place washers and wing nuts on the ends of the bolts to secure the backrest to the seat frame **(photo E).** Hand-tighten the wing nuts to lock the back-rest and legs in position. Loosen the wing nuts when you want to fold the lawn seat for transport or storage.

Trash Can Corral

*This two-sided structure keeps trash cans out of sight
but accessible from the curb or alley.*

CONSTRUCTION MATERIALS

Quantity	Lumber
3	2 × 4" × 6' cedar
2	2 × 2" × 10' cedar
1	1 × 8" × 2' cedar
7	1 × 6" × 10' cedar
8	1 × 4" × 8' cedar

Nothing ruins a view from a favorite window like the sight of trash cans—especially as garbage-collection day draws near. With this trash can corral, you'll see an attractive, freestanding cedar fence instead of unsightly trash cans.

The two fence-style panels support one another, so you don't need to set fence posts in the ground or in concrete. And because the collars at the bases of the posts can be adjusted, you can position the can corral on uneven or slightly sloping ground. The staggered panel slats hide the cans completely, but still allow air to pass through to ensure adequate ventilation.

OVERALL SIZE:
49¾" HIGH
49" WIDE
79" LONG

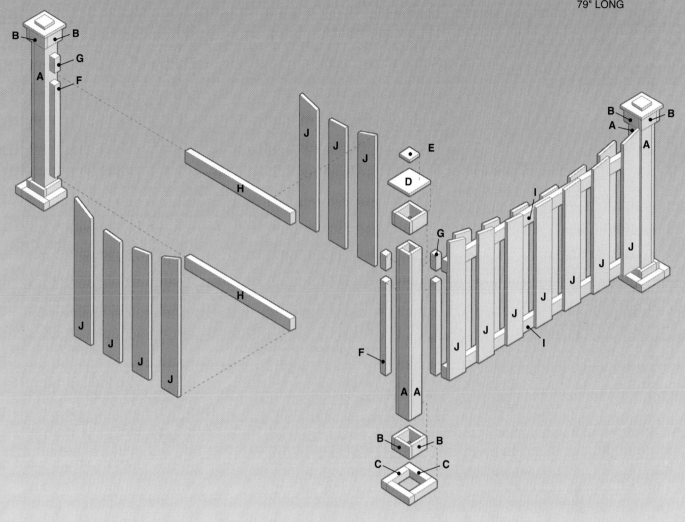

Cutting List

Key	Part	Dimension	Pcs.	Material
A	Post board	⅞ × 3½ × 48"	12	Cedar
B	Collar strip	⅞ × 3½ × 5¼"	24	Cedar
C	Foot strip	1½ × 1½ × 7⅝"	12	Cedar
D	Collar top	⅞ × 7¼ × 7¼"	3	Cedar
E	Collar cap	⅞ × 3½ × 3½"	3	Cedar

Cutting List

Key	Part	Dimension	Pcs.	Material
F	Long post cleat	1½ × 1½ × 26⅞"	4	Cedar
G	Short post cleat	1½ × 1½ × 4"	4	Cedar
H	Short stringer	1½ × 3½ × 35½"	2	Cedar
I	Long stringer	1½ × 3½ × 65½"	2	Cedar
J	Slat	⅞ × 5½ × 39½"	20	Cedar

Materials: 1½" and 2" deck screws, finishing materials.

Note: Measurements reflect the actual size of dimension lumber.

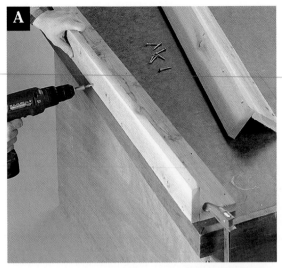

The post is made from four edge-joined boards.

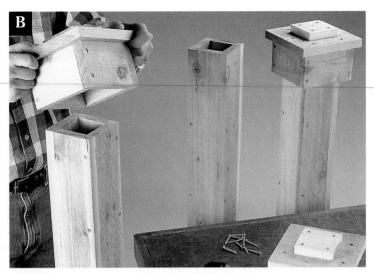

Fit the top collar assemblies onto each post and attach them.

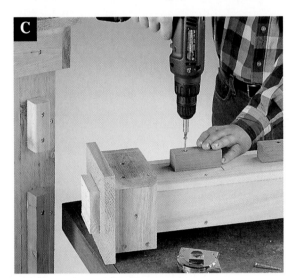

Attach the short post cleats 3⅜" up from the tops of the long post cleats. The top stringers on the panels fit between the cleats when installed.

Directions:
Trash Can Corral

BUILD THE POSTS.

Each post is made of four boards butted together to form a square.

1. Cut the post boards (A) to length and sand them smooth.
2. Clamp one post board to your work surface. Then, butt another post board against it at a right angle. With the ends flush, drill ⅛" pilot holes at 8" intervals and counterbore the holes to a ¼" depth. Connect the boards by driving 2" deck

screws through the pilot holes **(photo A).** Repeat the step until the post boards are fastened together in pairs. Then, fasten the pairs together to form the three posts.

MAKE AND ATTACH THE COLLARS.

Each post is wrapped at the top and bottom by a four-piece collar. The top collars have two-piece flat caps, and the base collars are wrapped with 2×2 strips for stability.

1. Cut the collar strips (B), collar tops (D) and collar caps (E) to size.
2. Join the collar strips together to form square frames, using 1½" deck screws.
3. Center each collar cap on top of a collar top, and attach the caps to the tops with 1½" deck screws.
4. To center the tops on the frames, mark lines on the bottoms of the top pieces, 1⅛" in from the edges. Then, drill pilot holes ½" in from the lines, and counterbore the holes.
5. Use the lines to center a frame under each top. Then, drive 1½" deck screws through the holes and into the frames.

6. Slip a top collar assembly over one end of each post **(photo B),** and drill centered pilot holes on each side of the collar. Counterbore the holes and drive 1½" deck screws into the posts.
7. Attach the remaining frames to the other ends of the posts, with the bottom edges flush.
8. Cut the foot strips (C) to length. Lay them around the bottoms of the base collars, and screw them together with 2" deck screws. Make sure the bottoms of the frames are flush with the bottoms of the collars. Then, attach the frames to the collars with 2" deck screws.

ATTACH THE CLEATS AND SUPPORTS.

The long and short post cleats (F, G) attach to the posts between and above the stringers.

1. Cut the post cleats to length. Center a long post cleat on one face of each post and attach it with 2" deck screws so the bottom is 4" above the top of the base collar on each post.
2. For the corner post, fasten a second long post cleat on an adjacent post face, 4" up from the bottom collar.

Use 4½"-wide spacers to set the gaps between panel slats.

Use a flexible guide to mark the top contours.

3. Center the short post cleats on the same post faces, 3⅝" up from the tops of the long post cleats. Attach the short post cleats to the posts, with 2" deck screws, making sure the short cleats are aligned with the long cleats **(photo C).**

BUILD THE FENCE PANELS.
1. Cut the short stringers (H), long stringers (I) and slats (J).
2. Position the short stringers on your work surface so they are parallel and separated by a 26⅞" gap. Attach a slat at each end of the stringers, so the ends of the stringers are flush with the outside edges of the slats. Drive a 1½" deck screw through each slat and into the face of each stringer.
3. Measure diagonally from corner to corner to make sure the fence panel is square. If the measurements are equal, the fence is square. If not, apply pressure to one side of the assembly until it is square. Drive another screw through each slat and into each stringer.
4. Cut 4½" spacers to set the gaps between panel slats, and attach the remaining slats on the same side of the stringers

by driving two 1½" deck screws at each end. Check that the bottoms of the slats are flush with the stringer **(photo D).**
5. Turn the panel over and attach slats to the other side, starting 4½" from the ends so slats on opposite sides are staggered—there will only be three slats on this side. Build the long panel the same way.

CONTOUR THE PANEL TOPS.
To lay out the curve at the top of each fence panel, you will need to make a marking guide.
1. Cut a thin, flexible strip of wood at least 6" longer than the long fence panel. On each panel, tack nails at the top outside corner of each end slat, and another nail midway across each panel, ½" above the top stringer.
2. Form a smooth curve by positioning the guide with the ends above the outside nails, and the midpoint below the nail in the center. Trace the contour onto the slats **(photo E),** and cut along the line with a jig saw. Use a short blade to avoid striking the slats on the other side. Use the same procedure on the other side of each

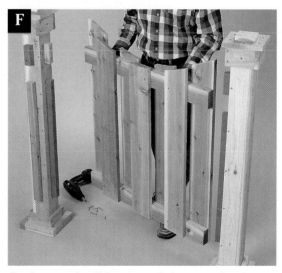

Set the completed fence panels between the cleats on the faces of the posts.

panel. Sand the cuts smooth.
3. Position the fence panels between the posts so the top stringer in each panel fits in the gap between the long and short post cleats **(photo F).** Drive 2" deck screws through the slats and into the cleats.

APPLY FINISHING TOUCHES.
Apply exterior wood stain to protect the cedar. You can increase the height of any of the posts slightly by detaching the base collar, lifting the post and reattaching the collar.

Trash Can Protector

Store that unsightly garbage can in this little structure to keep it hidden and safe from pests.

CONSTRUCTION MATERIALS

Quantity	Lumber
4	2" × 4 × 8' pine
1	¾" × 2 × 4' plywood
3	⅝" × 4 × 8' grooved siding
11	1 × 2" × 8' cedar

Anyone who has spent time at a cabin or a vacation home knows that garbage can storage can be a problem. Trash cans are not only ugly, they attract raccoons and other troublesome pests. Keep the trash out of sight and away from nighttime visitors with this simple trash can protector. It accommo-

dates a 44-gallon can and features a front and top that swing open for easy access. The 2 × 4 frame is paneled with grooved plywood siding. A cedar frame and cross rail stiffens each side panel and adds a decorative touch to the project. We used construction adhesive on this project because it adapts well to varying rates of expansion.

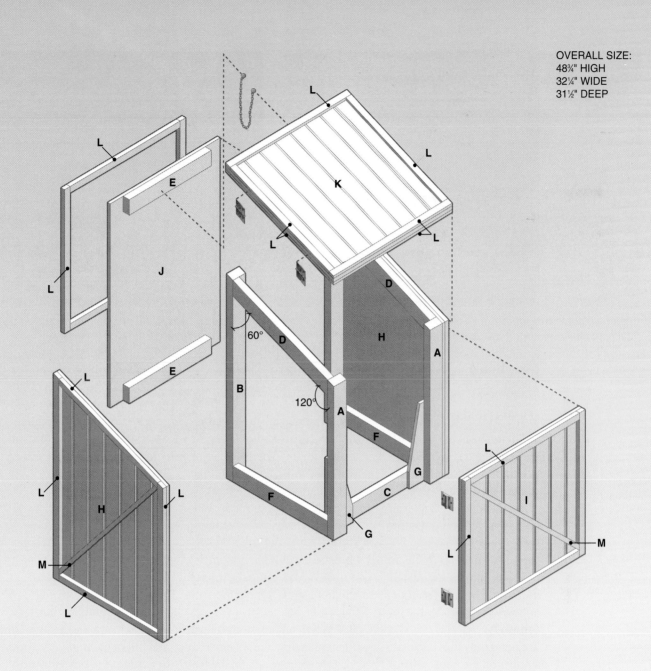

OVERALL SIZE:
48¾" HIGH
32¼" WIDE
31½" DEEP

Cutting List				
Key	Part	Dimension	Pcs.	Material
A	Front strut	1½ × 3½ × 36"	2	Pine
B	Back strut	1½ × 3½ × 46"	2	Pine
C	Front stringer	1½ × 3½ × 26¼"	1	Pine
D	Top rail	1½ × 3½ × 29¼"	2	Pine
E	Back stringer	1½ × 3½ × 22¼"	2	Pine
F	Bottom stringer	1½ × 3½ × 25½"	2	Pine
G	Brace	¾ × 6 × 16"	2	Plywood

Cutting List				
Key	Part	Dimension	Pcs.	Material
H	Side panel	⅝ × 29⅛ × 45¾"	2	Plywood siding
I	Front panel	⅝ × 32¼ × 34"	1	Plywood siding
J	Back panel	⅝ × 29¼ × 45¾"	1	Plywood siding
K	Top panel	⅝ × 33¾ × 32¼"	1	Plywood siding
L	Side batten	⅞ × 1½ × *	20	Cedar
M	Cross rail	⅞ × 1½ × *	3	Cedar

Materials: Construction adhesive, 1¼", 2" and 3" deck screws, 1" panhead screws (2), 6d galvanized finish nails, 3" × 3" utility hinges (2), 3" × 3" spring-loaded hinges (2), galvanized steel or plastic door pulls (2), steel chain (18"), finishing materials.

Note: Measurements reflect the actual size of dimension lumber.
*Cut to fit.

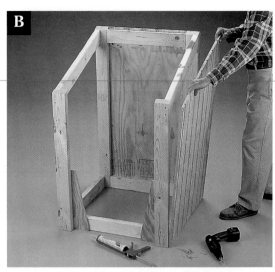

Center the back stringer flush with the bottom edge of the back before attaching it with screws and construction adhesive.

Attach side panels to the frame, making sure the front and top edges are flush with the frame.

Directions:
Trash Can Protector

MAKE THE BACK PANEL.
1. Cut the back panel (J) to size. Cut the back stringers (E) to length. Position one back stringer on the ungrooved face of the back panel, flush with the bottom edge. Center this back stringer so each end of the back stringer is 3½" in from the back panel sides. Attach the stringer with construction adhesive and 1¼" deck screws **(photo A).**
2. Center the other back stringer on the back panel, 1" down from the top edge. Attach it to the panel.

MAKE THE SIDE FRAMES.
1. Set a circular saw or a power miter box to cut at a 30° angle. Cut the front struts (A) and back struts (B) to length, making sure one end of each front and back strut is cut at a 30° angle. This slanted end cut should not affect the overall length of the struts (see *Diagram,* page 113).
2. Cut the bottom stringers (F) to length. Position the front

struts on edge on your work surface. Butt the end of a bottom stringer against each front strut. The outside faces of the bottom stringers should be flush with the outside edges of the front struts, and flush with the square ends of the front struts. Apply construction adhesive, and drive 3" deck screws through the front struts and into the ends of the bottom stringers. Make sure the tops of the front struts slant in the same direction.
3. Position a back strut against the unattached end of each bottom stringer. Attach them, making sure the slanted top ends of the back struts are facing the front struts.
4. Cut the top rails (D) to length. For the top rails to fit between the front and back struts, their ends must be cut at a 30° angle. When you cut the ends, make sure they are slanted in the correct directions. (First, check the struts and bottom stringer for square. Then, hold the top rails in place against the front and back struts, and trace the angle onto the top rails.)
5. Position the top rails be-

tween the front struts and back struts, making sure the outside faces are flush with the outside edges of the front struts and back struts. Attach the top rails with construction adhesive and 3" deck screws.

MAKE AND ATTACH THE SIDE BRACES.
1. Cut the braces (G) to size. Cut a slanted profile on the braces, so the top edge is 3" long and the bottom edge is 6" long. This slanted profile leaves room to move a garbage can in and out of the unit.
2. Position the braces against the inside faces of the front struts, making sure the braces butt against the bottom stringers. Fasten the braces with construction adhesive and 2" deck screws.

JOIN THE SIDES.
1. Cut the front stringer (C) to length. Stand the side frames up on your work surface so the front struts face the same direction. Position the front stringer between the side frames with one face abutting each brace.

Mark the ends of the cross rails before cutting them to fit between the frame corners.

ATTACH BATTENS AND CROSS RAILS.

The battens are pieces of trim that frame the panels. The cross rails fit diagonally from corner to corner on the side panels.

1. Measure the sides carefully before cutting the battens (L) to fit along the side and back panel edges. Be sure to cut side battens with the appropriate angle cuts. Fasten the battens to the side panels with construction adhesive and 6d finish nails.

2. Position the diagonal cross rails on the sides as shown so they span from corner to corner. Mark the angles required for the ends to fit snugly into the corners **(photo C).** Cut the cross rails to size and attach them.

3. Attach the battens to the back panel, making sure their outside and top edges are flush with the side faces and top edges of the rear side battens.

MAKE THE TOP AND FRONT PANELS.

1. Cut the top panel (K) and front panel (I) to size. Cut these parts from the same sheet of siding to make sure the grooves align on the finished project.

2. Cut and attach battens to frame the edges of the top panel on both faces.

3. Cut and attach battens and a cross rail on the front panel. Like the side panels, the front panel is framed on one face only and has a cross rail stretching from corner to corner.

4. Attach two spring-loaded, self-closing hinges to the front panel, and mount it on the front of the project. The bottom edge of the front panel should be 1" up from the bottoms of the stringers. Mount the top panel with two 3" × 3" utility hinges **(photo D).**

5. Attach handles or pulls on the front and top of the garbage can holder. Use two panhead screws to attach an 18"-long safety chain to the front face of the top back stringer and top panel to keep the top panel from swinging open too far. Fasten the ends of the chain 10" in from the hinged edge of the top panel.

6. Finish the trash can protector with an exterior-rated stain. If pests are a problem, attach latches to the front and top to hold them in place.

2. Make sure the ends of the front stringer are in contact with the bottom stringers. Attach the front stringer, using construction adhesive and 3" deck screws.

COMPLETE THE FRAME.

1. Position the back panel against the back of the frame sides. Make sure the back stringers are flush between the back struts, and attach the back panel to the frame with construction adhesive and 1¼" deck screws. The side edges of the back should be flush with the frame sides.

2. Cut the side panels (H) to size. Set them against the frame sides, making sure the front and back edges align and the panel rests squarely on the ground.

3. Trace the top edge of the frame onto the back (ungrooved) face of the side panels. Cut along the line with a circular saw. Attach the side panels with construction adhesive and 1¼" deck screws **(photo B).**

Mount the top to the top of a side panel with 3" × 3" utility hinges.

Front-Porch Mailbox

This cedar mailbox is a practical, good-looking project that is very easy to build. The simple design is created using basic joinery and mostly straight cuts.

If you want to build a useful, long-lasting item in just a few hours, this mailbox is the project for you. Replace that impersonal metal mailbox you bought at the hardware store with a distinctive cedar mailbox that's a lot of fun to build. The lines and design are so simple on this project that it suits nearly any home entrance. The mailbox features a hinged lid and a convenient lower shelf that is sized to hold magazines and newspapers.

We used select cedar to build our mailbox, then applied a clear, protective finish. Plain brass house numbers dress up the flat surface of the lid, which also features a decorative scallop that doubles as a handgrip.

If you are ambitious and economy-minded, you can build this entire mailbox using just one 8'-long piece of 1 × 10 cedar. That means, however, that you'll have to do quite a bit of rip-cutting to make the parts. If you have a good straightedge and some patience, rip-cutting is not difficult. But you may prefer to simply purchase dimensional lumber that matches the widths of the pieces (see the *Construction Materials* list to the left).

If your house is sided with wood siding, you can hang the mailbox by screwing the back directly to the siding. If you have vinyl or metal siding, be sure that the screws make it all the way through the siding and into wood sheathing or wood wall studs. If you have masonry siding, like brick or stucco, use masonry anchors to hang the mailbox.

CONSTRUCTION MATERIALS

Quantity	Lumber
1	1 × 10" × 4' cedar
1	1 × 8" × 3' cedar
1	1 × 4" × 3' cedar
1	1 × 3" × 3' cedar
1	1 × 2" × 3' cedar

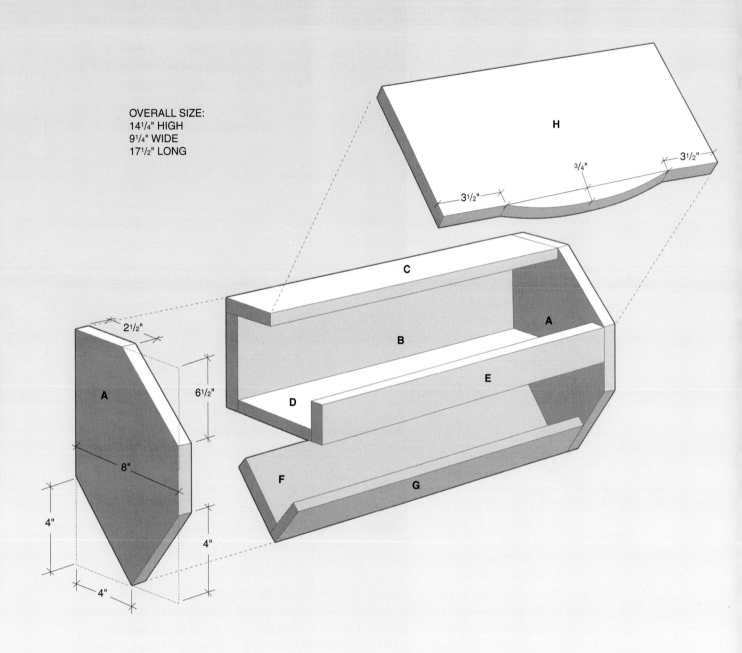

OVERALL SIZE:
14¼" HIGH
9¼" WIDE
17½" LONG

Cutting List				
Key	**Part**	**Dimension**	**Pcs.**	**Material**
A	Side	¾ × 8 × 14¼"	2	Cedar
B	Back	¾ × 7¼ × 16"	1	Cedar
C	Top	¾ × 2½ × 16"	1	Cedar
D	Box bottom	¾ × 6½ × 16"	1	Cedar

Cutting List				
Key	**Part**	**Dimension**	**Pcs.**	**Material**
E	Box front	¾ × 1½ × 16"	1	Cedar
F	Shelf bottom	¾ × 3½ × 16"	1	Cedar
G	Shelf lip	¾ × 2½ × 16"	1	Cedar
H	Lid	¾ × 9¼ × 17½"	1	Cedar

Materials: Moisture-resistant wood glue, 2" deck screws, masking tape, piano hinge with screws, finishing materials.

Note: Measurements reflect the actual size of dimension lumber.

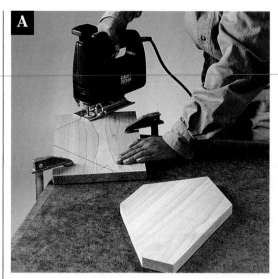

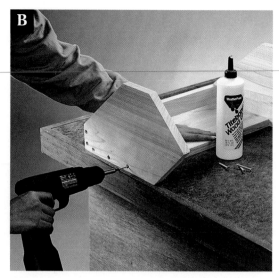

Cutlines are drawn on the sides, and the parts are cut to shape with a jig saw.

After fastening the top between the sides, fasten the back with deck screws.

Directions:
Front-Porch Mailbox

BUILD THE SIDES.

The sides are the trickiest parts to build in this mailbox design. But if you can use a ruler and cut a straight line, you should have no problems.

1. Cut two 8" × 14¼" pieces to make the sides (A).

2. Pieces of wood that will be shaped into parts are called "blanks" in the woodworkers' language. Lay out the cutting pattern onto one side blank, using the measurements shown on page 117. Mark all of the cutting lines, then double-check the dimensions to make sure the piece will be the right size when it is cut to shape. Make the cuts in the blank, using a jig saw, to create one side. Sand edges smooth.

3. Use this side as a template to mark the second blank.

Attach the box bottom to the back with glue and screws driven through the back and sides.

Arrange the template so the grain direction is the same in the blank and the template. Cut out and sand the second side **(photo A).**

ATTACH THE BACK AND TOP.

Fasten all the pieces on the mailbox with exterior wood glue and 2" deck screws. Although cedar is a fine outdoor wood, it can be quite brittle. To prevent splitting, drill ⅛" pilot holes and counterbore the holes ¼" deep, using a counter-bore bit. Space the screws evenly when driving them.

1. Cut the back (B) and top (C) to length. Fasten the top between the 2½"-wide faces on the two sides with glue and 2" deck screws. Position the top so that the rear face is flush with the rear side edges, and the top face is flush with the top side edges.

2. Use glue and deck screws to fasten the back between the sides, flush with the 10¼"-long edges **(photo B),** and butted against the top.

Keep the lip edges flush with the side edges to form the newspaper shelf.

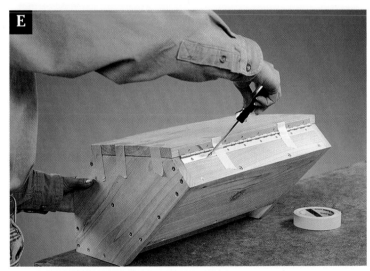

Once the pieces are taped in place, the continuous hinge is attached to join the lid to the top.

ATTACH THE BOX BOTTOM AND FRONT.

The bottom and front pieces form the letter compartment inside the mailbox.

1. Cut the bottom (D) and front (E) to length. Fasten the bottom to the back and sides, making sure the bottom edges are flush **(photo C).**

2. Once the bottom is attached, fasten the front to the sides and bottom, keeping the bottom edges flush.

ATTACH THE NEWSPAPER SHELF.

The lower shelf on the underside of the mailbox is designed for overflow mail.

1. To make the lower shelf, cut the shelf bottom (F) and shelf lip (G) to size. Fasten the shelf lip to the leg of the "V" formed by the sides that are closer to the front.

2. Fasten the shelf bottom to the sides along the back edges to complete the shelf assembly **(photo D).**

CUT AND ATTACH THE LID.

1. Cut the lid (H) to length (9¼" is the actual width of a 1 × 10). Draw a reference line parallel to and ¾" away from one of the long edges.

2. With a jig saw, make a 3½"-long cut at each end of the line. Mark the midpoint of the edge (8¾"), then cut a shallow scallop to connect the cuts with the midpoint. Smooth out the cut with a sander.

3. Attach a brass, 15"-long continuous hinge known as a piano hinge to the top edge of the lid. Then position the lid so the other wing of the hinge fits squarely onto the top of the mailbox. Secure the lid to the mailbox with masking tape. Attach the hinge to the mailbox **(photo E).**

APPLY FINISHING TOUCHES.

1. Sand all surfaces smooth with 150-grit sandpaper.

2. Finish the mailbox with a clear wood sealer or other finish of your choice. Add 3" brass house numbers on the lid. Or, stencil an address or name onto it (see *Tips*, page 118). Once the finish has dried, hang the mailbox on the wall by driving screws through the back.

TIP

Clear wood sealer can be refreshed if it starts to yellow or peel. Wash the wood with a strong detergent, then sand the surface lightly to remove flaking or peeling sealer. Wash the surface again, then simply brush a fresh coat of sealer onto the wood.

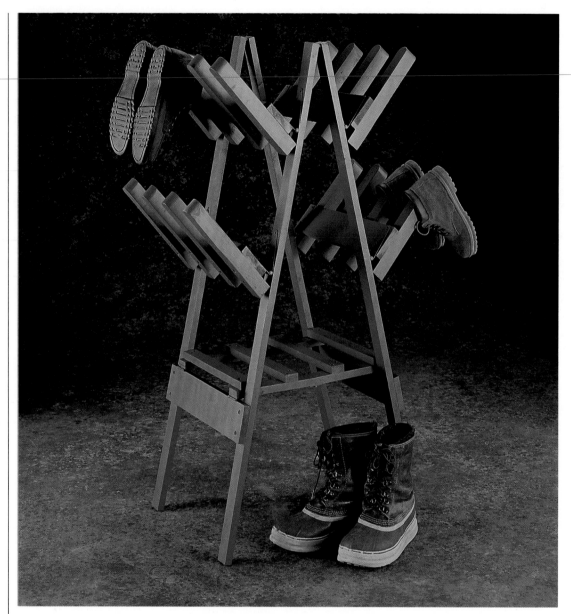

Boot Dryer

Hiking or biking, skiing or just working outdoors, nothing beats the feeling of slipping into a pair of warm, dry boots.

CONSTRUCTION MATERIALS

Quantity	Lumber
4	1 × 2" × 8' pine
1	1 × 4" × 8' pine
2	2 × 2" × 8' pine

You may not want to display this boot dryer in the middle of your cabin when company arrives. But if you've ever had to don a pair of damp boots on a cold morning, you'll appreciate the speed with which boots dry when they're suspended on our boot dryer.

The boot spindles keep boots (as many as eight pairs at a time) in their optimal drying position, well above the ground. The open design leaves plenty of space for air to circulate. For fast drying, set the boot dryer near a heat register or in a room with a fireplace.

When it's is not in use, the boot dryer folds flat for storage in just about any closet.

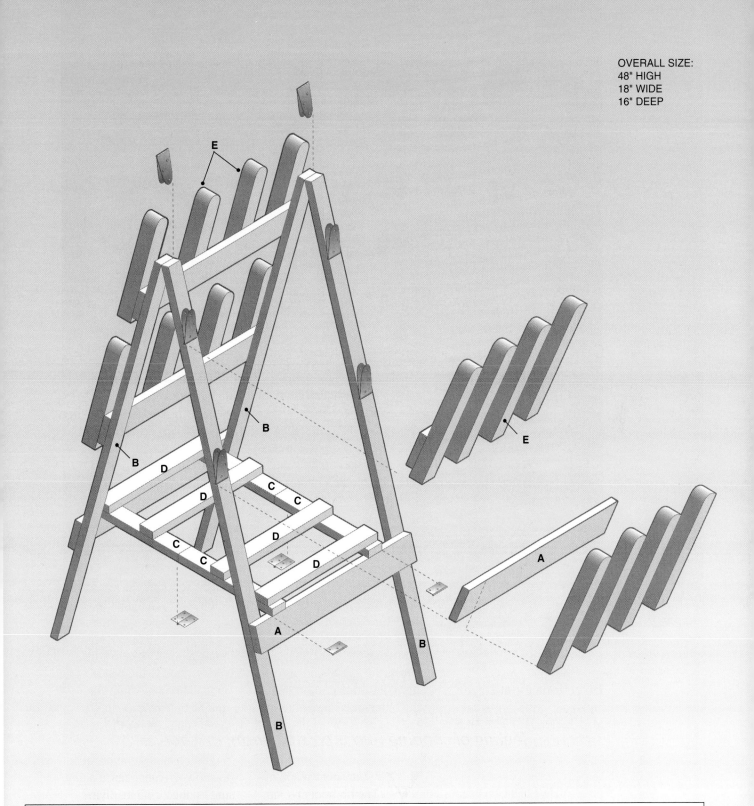

Cutting List				
Key	**Part**	**Dimension**	**Pcs.**	**Material**
A	Hinge rail	¾ × 3½ × 15⅞"	6	Pine
B	Leg	¾ × 1½ × 49"	4	Pine
C	Center slat	¾ × 1½ × 9"	4	Pine

Cutting List				
Key	**Part**	**Dimension**	**Pcs.**	**Material**
D	Cross slat	¾ × 1½ × 12½"	4	Pine
E	Boot spindle	1½ × 1½ × 11⅞"	16	Pine

Materials: Moisture-resistant glue, #6 × ¾" and #6 × 2" wood screws, 1½ × 3" strap hinges (10), 1½ × 1½" butt hinges (6).

Note: Measurements reflect the actual size of dimension lumber.

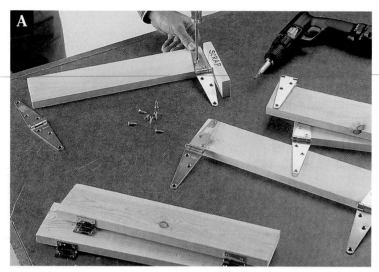

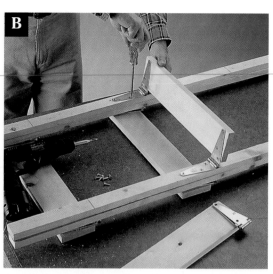

Use a piece of scrap wood as a stop to help you align the strap hinge barrels so they are flush with the ends of the hinge rails.

Attach the top hinge rails to the legs so their bottom edges are flush with the reference lines.

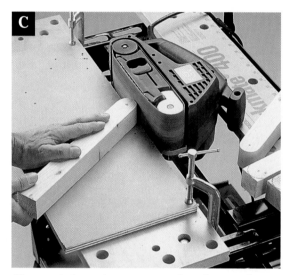

Clamp a belt sander to your work surface, and round one end of each boot spindle.

Directions: Boot Dryer

MAKE THE HINGE RAILS.
1. Cut the hinge rails (A) to length. Sand rough spots smooth. Fasten pairs of butt hinges to two of the hinge rails, using #6 × ¾" wood screws. Attach the butt hinges along one edge of each board, 1⅝" in from each end. The hinge barrels should not overhang the edges of the rails.
2. Position a pair of heavy-duty strap hinges on one face of each of the four remaining

hinge rails. Check that the hinges are flush with the ends of the rails by pressing a piece of scrap wood against the end of each rail to make stops for the hinges. Fasten the strap hinges to the four hinge rails with #6 × ¾" wood screws **(photo A).**

MAKE THE LEGS.
1. Cut the legs (B) to length and sand them smooth. Position them against each other, edge to edge on your work surface. With the ends of the legs flush, draw reference lines across the legs 8" and 21½" in from one end, and 14½" in from the other end. These lines mark the positions for the hinge rails.
2. Butt the ends of two legs together and attach a strap hinge over the joint, using wood screws. The barrel of the strap hinge should face away from the legs. Repeat the step to make the other leg pair.

ATTACH TOP HINGE RAILS.
1. Fold the leg pairs into the closed position and place them 16" apart on your work surface.
2. Position the hinge rails with

the attached strap hinges so their bottom edges are flush with the top two reference lines (8" and 21½") on the legs. Attach the free hinge plates **(photo B).** The hinge rails should fold upward against the legs when they are attached.

MAKE THE BOOT SPINDLES.
1. Cut the boot spindles (E) to length. To round the tips of the spindles, draw a ¾"-radius curve at one end of each spindle, using a compass as a guide. Clamp a belt sander to your work surface so the belt is vertical. Use a medium-grit sanding belt to shape the spindle ends **(photo C).** Repeat the step for the other spindles.
2. Position a boot spindle at one end of a hinge rail, making sure its outside edge is flush with the end of the hinge rail. The bottom of the spindle should extend 1½" below the bottom edge of the hinge rail. (You can draw reference lines 1½" up from the bottoms of the spindles to help you position them correctly.) Drill two ⅛" pilot holes in the spindle. Coun-

terbore the holes to a ¼" depth, using a counterbore bit. Attach the spindle to the hinge rail with glue and #6 × 2" wood screws.

3. Attach the rest of the spindles (see *Diagram*, page 121) evenly spaced, about 3¼" apart. Use a 3¼"-wide piece of scrap wood as a gauge **(photo D)**.

MAKE THE SHELF.

The shelf in the bottom of the boot dryer is designed to provide a convenient place for shoes and other items while enhancing the boot dryer's stability. When the dryer is completed, the shelf will fold out between the leg pairs as the legs are extended, and fold flat when the legs are collapsed.

1. Cut the center slats (C) and cross slats (D) to length.

2. Arrange the center slats in pairs so their ends are flush. With the center slats positioned edge to edge, draw reference lines ½" and 5½" in from one end of each slat.

3. Set a pair of cross slats on the center slat pairs so the outside edge of each cross slat is flush with the reference lines. Adjust the positions of the center slats so the ends of the cross slats are flush with the edges of the center slats.

4. Drill pilot holes in the cross slats and counterbore the holes. Attach the cross slats with glue and drive #6 × 1¼" wood screws through the cross slats and into the center slats.

5. Turn the two frames upside down so the cross slats are on your work surface. Butt them together so the ½"-wide gap is on the outside. Join the frames with butt hinges. The barrels of the hinges should face away from the center slats. Remove the hinges for now.

6. Position the remaining hinge rails on the legs so their top edges are flush with the reference lines, 14½" up from the bottoms of the legs. Make sure the hinges are on the top edge of the hinge rails, with the barrels facing out. Fasten the hinge rails to the legs with glue and #6 × 1¼" wood screws.

7. Set the frame on its side. Attach the shelf frames to the hinge rails, fastening the unattached hinge plates to the center slats. (The hinges should be attached to the center slat faces opposite the cross slats.) Fold the shelf frames between the legs, and reattach them with butt hinges **(photo E)**.

Use a piece of scrap to maintain even spacing as you attach the boot spindles to the hinge rails.

APPLY FINISHING TOUCHES.

Open and close the boot rack to make sure it operates correctly. Finish the boot dryer with primer and enamel paint. Or, for an attractive natural look, apply a clear protective finish, such as polyurethane, to the wood.

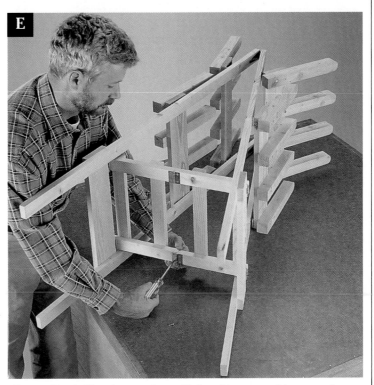

Fasten the shelf racks together with butt hinges, making sure the hinge barrels are facing the bottoms of the legs.

Outdoor Occasional Table

The traditional design of this deck table provides a stylishly simple addition to any porch, deck or patio.

CONSTRUCTION MATERIALS

Quantity	Lumber
2	1 × 3" × 8' cedar
6	1 × 4" × 8' cedar

Create a functional yet stylish accent for your porch, deck or patio with this cedar deck table. This table makes an ideal surface for serving cold lemonade on hot summer days, a handy place to set your plate during a family cookout, or simply a comfortable place to rest your feet after a long day. Don't be fooled by its lightweight design and streamlined features—the little table is extremely sturdy. Structural features such as middle and end stringers tie the aprons and legs together and transfer weight from the table slats to the legs. This attractive little table is easy to build and will provide many years of durable service.

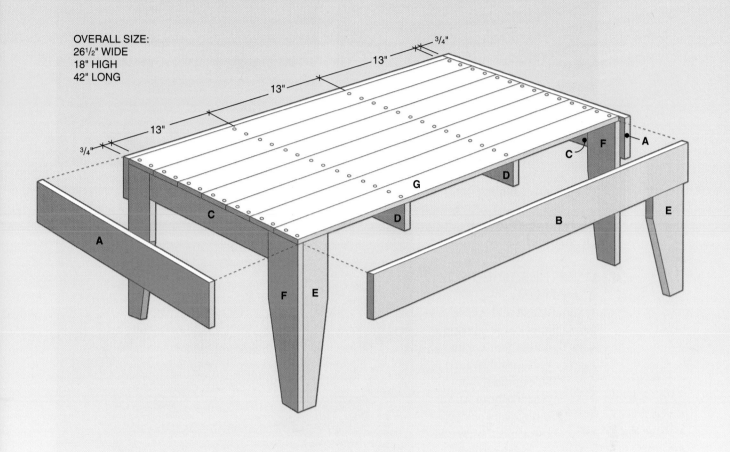

OVERALL SIZE:
26½" WIDE
18" HIGH
42" LONG

Cutting List				
Key	**Part**	**Dimension**	**Pcs.**	**Material**
A	End apron	¾ × 3½ × 26½"	2	Cedar
B	Side apron	¾ × 3½ × 40½"	2	Cedar
C	End stringer	¾ × 2½ × 18"	2	Cedar
D	Middle stringer	¾ × 2½ × 25"	2	Cedar

Cutting List				
Key	**Part**	**Dimension**	**Pcs.**	**Material**
E	Narrow leg side	¾ × 2½ × 17¼"	4	Cedar
F	Wide leg side	¾ × 3½ × 17¼"	4	Cedar
G	Slat	¾ × 3½ × 40½"	7	Cedar

Materials: Moisture-resistant glue, 1¼" deck screws.

Note: Measurements reflect the actual size of dimension lumber.

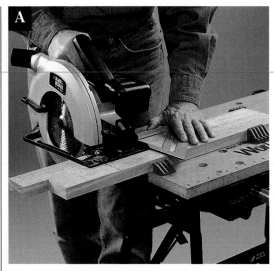

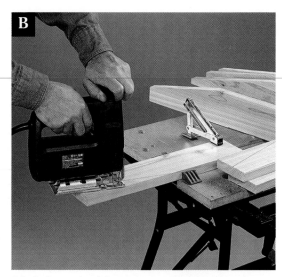

Use a speed square as a cutting guide and gang-cut the table parts when possible for uniform results.

Mark the ends of the tapers on the leg sides, then connect the marks to make taper cutting lines.

Directions: Outdoor Occasional Table

MAKE THE STRINGERS AND APRONS.

1. The stringers and aprons form a frame for the tabletop slats. To make them, cut the end aprons (A) and side aprons (B) to length **(photo A).** For fast, straight cutting, use a speed square as a saw guide—the flange on the speed square hooks over the edge of the boards to hold it securely in place while you cut.

2. Cut the end stringers (C) and middle stringers (D) to length.

MAKE THE LEG PARTS.

1. Cut the narrow leg sides (E) and wide leg sides (F) to length.

2. On one wide leg side piece, measure 8¾" along one edge of the leg side and place a mark. Measure across the bottom end of the leg side 1½" and place a

TIP

Rip-cut cedar 1 × 4s to 2½" in width if you are unable to find good clear cedar 1 × 3s (nominal). When rip-cutting, always use a straightedge guide for your circular saw. A straight piece of lumber clamped to your workpiece makes an adequate guide, or buy a metal straight-edge guide with built-in clamps.

Use a jig saw or circular saw to cut the leg tapers.

mark. Connect the two marks to create a cutting line for the leg taper. Mark cutting lines for the tapers on all four wide leg sides **(photo B).**

3. On the thin leg sides, measure 8¾" along an edge and ¾" across the bottom end to make endpoints for the taper cutting lines.

4. Clamp each leg side to your work surface. Cut along the taper cutoff line, using a jig saw or circular saw, to create the tapered leg sides **(photo C).** Sand all leg parts smooth.

ASSEMBLE THE LEG PAIRS.

1. Apply a ½"-wide layer of moisture-resistant glue on the face of a wide leg side, next to the untapered edge. Then apply a thin layer of glue to the untapered edge of a narrow leg side. Join the leg sides together at a right angle to form a leg pair. Reinforce the joint with 1¼" deck screws.

2. Glue and screw the rest of the leg pairs in the same manner **(photo D).** Be careful not to use too much glue. Excess glue can get messy and could

Fasten the leg pairs by driving deck screws through the face of the wide side and into the narrow edge.

Test the layout of the slats before you fasten them, adjusting as necessary to make sure gaps are even.

cause problems later if you plan to stain or clear-coat the finish.

MAKE THE TABLETOP FRAME.

1. Fasten the side aprons (B) to the leg pairs with glue and screws. Be sure to screw from the back side of the leg pair and into the side aprons so the screw heads will be concealed. The narrow leg side of each pair should be facing in toward the center of the side apron, with the outside faces of the wide leg sides flush with the ends of the side apron. The tops of the leg pairs should be ¾" down from the tops of the side aprons to create recesses for the tabletop slats.
2. Attach the end aprons (A) to the leg assemblies with glue. Drive screws from the back side of the leg pairs. Make sure the end aprons are positioned so the ends are flush with the outside faces of the side aprons.
3. Attach the end stringers (C) to the end aprons between the leg pairs with glue. Drive the screws from the back sides of the end stringers and into the end aprons.

4. Cut the middle stringers (D) to length. Measure 13" in from the inside face of each end stringer and mark reference lines on the side aprons for positioning the middle stringers.
5. Use glue to attach the middle stringers to the side aprons—centered on the reference lines. Drive deck screws through the side aprons and into the ends of the middle stringers. Make sure the middle stringers are positioned ¾" down from the tops of the side aprons.

CUT AND INSTALL THE SLATS.

1. Before you cut the slats (G), measure the inside dimension between the end aprons to be sure that the slat length is correct. Then cut the slats to length, using a circular saw and a speed square to keep the cuts square. It is extremely important to make square cuts on the ends of the slats since they're going to be the most visible cuts on the entire table.
2. Run a bead of glue along the top faces of the middle and end stringers. Screw the slats to

the stringers leaving a gap of approximately ¹⁄₁₆" between each of the individual slats **(photo E).**

APPLY FINISHING TOUCHES.

1. Smooth all sharp edges by using a router with a roundover bit or a power sander with medium-grit (#100 to 120) sandpaper. Finish-sand the entire table and clean off the sanding residue.
2. Apply a finish, such as clear wood sealer. If you want, fill any screw counterbores with tinted wood putty.

TIP

Clamp all workpiece parts whenever possible during the assembly process. Clamping will hold glued-up and squared-up parts securely in place until you permanently fasten them with screws. Large, awkward assemblies will be more manageable with the help of a few clamps.

Park Bench

This attention-grabbing park bench is a real showpiece that can transform even a plain yard into a formal garden.

CONSTRUCTION MATERIALS

Quantity	Lumber
5	2 × 4" × 8' pine
1	2 × 2" × 4' pine
4	1 × 6" × 8' pine

Add color and style to your backyard or garden with this bright, elegant park bench. Some careful jig saw work is all it takes to make the numerous curves and contours that give this bench a sophisticated look. But don't worry if your cuts aren't all perfect—the shapes are decorative, so the bench will still

work just fine. In fact, if you prefer a simpler appearance, you can build the park bench with all straight parts, except the roundovers at the bottoms of the legs. But if you are willing to do the extra work, you're sure to be pleased with the final result. You may even want to finish it with bright red paint so no one will miss it.

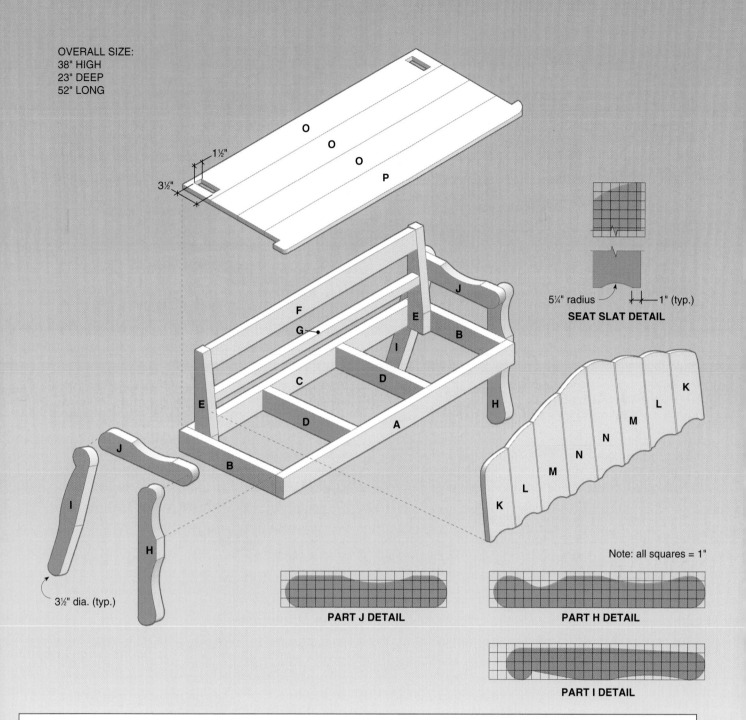

OVERALL SIZE:
38" HIGH
23" DEEP
52" LONG

1½"

3½"

5¼" radius — 1" (typ.)

SEAT SLAT DETAIL

Note: all squares = 1"

3½" dia. (typ.)

PART J DETAIL

PART H DETAIL

PART I DETAIL

Cutting List				
Key	**Part**	**Dimension**	**Pcs.**	**Material**
A	Front rail	1½ × 3½ × 49"	1	Pine
B	Side rail	1½ × 3½ × 20¼"	2	Pine
C	Back rail	1½ × 3½ × 46"	1	Pine
D	Cross rail	1½ × 3½ × 18¾"	2	Pine
E	Post	1½ × 3½ × 18"	2	Pine
F	Top rail	1½ × 3½ × 43"	1	Pine
G	Bottom rail	1½ × 1½ × 43"	1	Pine
H	Front leg	1½ × 3½ × 24½"	2	Pine

Cutting List				
Key	**Part**	**Dimension**	**Pcs.**	**Material**
I	Rear leg	1½ × 3½ × 23"	2	Pine
J	Armrest	1½ × 3½ × 18½"	2	Pine
K	End slat	¾ × 5½ × 14"	2	Pine
L	Outside slat	¾ × 5½ × 16"	2	Pine
M	Inside slat	¾ × 5½ × 18"	2	Pine
N	Center slat	¾ × 5½ × 20"	2	Pine
O	Seat slat	¾ × 5½ × 49"	3	Pine
P	Seat nose slat	¾ × 5½ × 52"	1	Pine

Materials: Moisture-resistant glue, 1¼", 2½" deck screws, finishing materials.

Note: All measurements reflect the actual size of dimension lumber.

Use a router or sander to round over the sharp bottom edges and corners of the completed seat frame.

Attach the seat slats and nose slat to the top of the seat frame with glue and deck screws.

Directions: Park Bench

BUILD THE SEAT FRAME.
The seat frame is made by assembling rails and cross rails to form a rectangular unit.

1. Cut the front rail (A), side rails (B), back rail (C) and cross rails (D) to length. Sand rough spots with medium-grit sandpaper.

2. Fasten the side rails to the front rail with moisture-resistant glue. Drill ⅛" pilot holes in the front rail. Counterbore the holes to accept ⅜"-dia. wood plugs. Drive 2½" deck screws through the front rail and into the side rail ends. Make sure the top and bottom edges of the side rails are flush with the top and bottom edges of the front rail.

3. Attach the back rail between the side rails. Drill pilot holes in the side rails. Counterbore the holes. Fasten with glue and drive screws through the side rails and into the ends of the back rail. Keep the back rail flush with the ends of the side rails.

4. Use glue and deck screws to fasten the two cross rails between the front and back rails, 14½" in from the inside face of each side rail.

5. Complete the seat frame by rounding the bottom edges and corners with a router and a ⅜"-dia. roundover bit **(photo A)** or a hand sander.

MAKE THE SEAT SLATS.
The seat nose slat has side cutouts to accept the front legs. The back seat slat has cutouts, called mortises, to accept the posts that support the backrest.

1. Cut the seat nose slat (P) and one seat slat (O) to length. To mark the 2 × 4 cutouts, use the end of a 2 × 4 as a template.

> **TIP**
>
> *Making smooth contour cuts with a jig saw can be a little tricky. To make it easier, install fairly thick saw blades, because they are less likely to "wander" with the grain of the wood. Using a scrolling jig saw will also help, since they are easier to turn than standard jig saws.*

2. Position the 2 × 4 on the seat slat at each end, 1½" in from the back edge and 1½" in from the end. The long sides of the 2 × 4 should be parallel to the ends of the back seat slat. Trace the outline of the 2 × 4 onto the slat. Drill a starter hole within the outline on the back seat slat. Make the cutout with a jig saw.

3. Use a jig saw to cut a 3"-long × 1½"-wide notch at each end of the nose slat, starting at the back edge (see *Diagram*, page 129). Sand the notches and mortises with a file or a thin sanding block. Use a router with roundover bit to shape the front edge of the nose slat.

ATTACH THE SEAT SLATS.

1. Cut the rest of the seat slats (O) to length. Lay the slats on the seat frame so the ends of the slats are flush with the frame, and the nose slat overhangs equally at the sides of the frame.

2. Draw reference lines

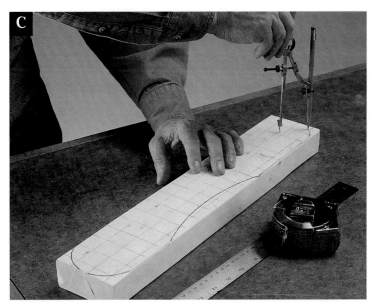

After drawing a 1" grid on the legs and armrests, draw the finished shape of the parts, following the Grid Patterns on page 129.

onto the tops of the seat slats and nose slat, directly over the top of each rail in the frame. Mark two drilling points on each slat on each line—on all but the front of the nose slat. Points should be ¾" in from the front and back of the slats. On the nose slat, mark drilling points 1½" in from the front of the slat. Drill pilot holes and counterbore the holes.

3. Sand the seat slats and nose slat. Attach them to the seat frame with glue. Drive 1¼" deck screws through the slats and into the frame and cross rails **(photo B).** Start with the front and back slats, and space the inner slats evenly.

MAKE THE LEGS AND ARMRESTS.
The front legs (H), rear legs (I) and armrests (J) are shaped using the grid patterns on page 129.

1. Cut workpieces for the parts to the full sizes shown in the *Cutting List.* Use a pencil to draw a 1"-square grid pattern on each workpiece.

2. Using the grid patterns as a reference, draw the shapes onto the workpieces **(photo C).** (It will help if you enlarge the patterns on a photocopier or draw them to a larger scale on a piece of graph paper first.)

3. Cut out the shapes with a jig saw. Sand the contour cuts smooth. Use a drum sander mounted in your electric drill for best results.

ATTACH THE LEGS.
The front and rear legs are attached to the armrests, flush with the front and rear ends.

1. Fasten the front legs to the outside faces of the armrests. Drill pilot holes in the legs. Counterbore the holes. Drive deck screws through the holes

and into the armrests. Use a framing square to make sure the legs are perpendicular to the armrests.

2. Temporarily fasten the rear legs to the outside faces of the armrests by drilling centered pilot holes and driving a screw through each rear leg and into the armrest. The rear leg must, for now, remain adjustable.

3. Clamp the seat to the legs. The front of the edge of the seat should be 16¾" up from the bottoms of the front legs. The back of the seat should be 14¼" up from the bottoms of the rear legs. Position square wood spacers between the seat and each armrest to keep the armrest parallel to the frame.

4. Adjust the rear legs so their back edges are flush with the top corners of the side rails. The rear legs extend slightly beyond the back of the seat frame.

5. Drill pilot holes in the front and rear legs. Counterbore the holes. Drive deck screws through the front and rear legs and into the side. Drive an additional screw through each

Carefully clamp the leg frames to the seat, and attach them with glue and screws, driven through centered, counterbored pilot holes.

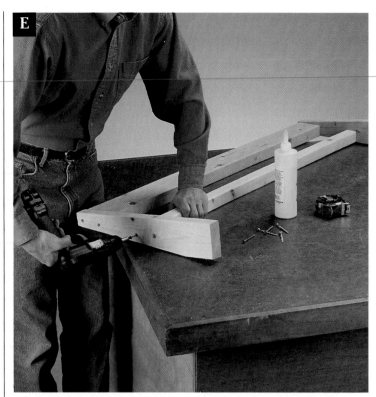

Glue the ends of the top and bottom rails, then drive deck screws through the posts to attach them to the rails.

rear leg into the armrests to secure the rear legs in position.

6. Unclamp the leg assemblies, and remove them from the frame **(photo D).** Apply glue to the leg assemblies where they join the frame and reattach the legs and armrests using the same screw holes.

BUILD THE BACK FRAME.

The back frame is made by attaching a top rail (F) and bottom rail (G) between two posts (E). Once the back frame has been built, it is inserted into the mortises in the rear seat slats. Tapers cut on the front edges of the posts will create a backward slope so the back slats (make a more comfortable backrest.) When you attach the rails between the posts, make sure they are flush with the front edges of the posts.

1. Cut the posts, top rail and bottom rail to length. Mark a tapered cutting line on each post, starting 1½" in from the back edge, at the top. Extend the line so it meets the front edge 3½" up from the bottom. Cut the taper in each post, using a circular saw or jig saw.

2. Use glue and deck screws to fasten the top rail between the posts so the front face of the top rail is flush with the front (tapered) edge of each post. The top front corner of the top rail should be flush with the top of the posts.

3. Position the bottom rail between the posts so its bottom edge is 9" up from the bottoms of the posts. Make sure the front face of the bottom rail is flush with the front edges of the posts. Drill pilot holes in the posts. Counterbore the holes. Attach the parts with glue and 2½" deck screws **(photo E).** Use a router with a ⅜"-dia. roundover bit or a hand sander to round over the back edges of the back frame.

MAKE THE BACK SLATS.

The back slats are shaped on their tops and bottoms to create a scalloped effect. If you'd rather not spend the time cutting these contours, you can simply cut the slats to length and round over the top edges.

1. Cut the end slats (K), outside slats (L), inside slats (M) and center slats (N) to length. Draw a 1"-square grid pattern on one slat. Then, draw the shape shown in the back slat detail on page 129 onto the slat. Use a compass to mark a 5¼"-radius scalloped cutout at the bottom of the slat.

2. Cut the slat to shape with a jig saw and sand smooth.

3. Use the completed slat as a template to trace the same profile on the tops and bottoms of the remaining slats **(photo F).** Cut them to shape with a jig saw and sand the cuts smooth.

ATTACH THE BACK SLATS.

1. Before attaching the back slats to the back frame, clamp a straight board across the fronts of the posts with its top edge 8½" up from the bottoms of the posts **(photo G).** Use this board as a guide to keep the slats aligned as you attach them.

2. Fasten the end slats to the

TIP

Depending on the location of your yard and garden furnishings, you may encounter some uneven terrain. If the ground is hard, you can install adjustable leveler glides to the bottoms of the legs to keep your projects level. If the project is resting on softer ground, the easiest solution is to use flat stones to shim under the lower sides or legs. Or, you can throw down a loose-stone base under the project, and tamp it until it is level.

Use the first completed back slat as a template for tracing cutting lines on the rest of the back slats.

Clamp a straight board to the back frame to help keep the back slats aligned along their bottom edges as you install them.

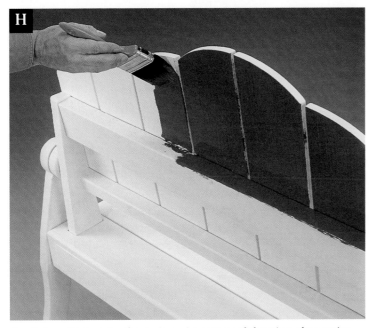

Apply two thin coats of exterior primer to seal the pine, then paint the park bench with two coats of enamel house trim paint.

back frame with glue and deck screws, making sure the bottoms are resting flat against the clamped guide board. (For more information on back slat positioning, see the *Diagram*, page 129.) Make sure the outside edges of the end slats are flush with the outside edges of the posts.

3. Attach the remaining slats between the end slats, spaced so the gaps are even.

ASSEMBLE THE BENCH.

1. Attach the rear frame by sliding the back into place inside the notches in the rear seat slat. The posts should rest against the back rail and side rails.

Keep the bottoms of the posts flush with the bottom edges of the side rails.

2. Drill pilot holes in the posts and the back rail. Counterbore the holes. Drive 2½" screws through the posts and into the side rails, and through the back rail and into the posts.

APPLY FINISHING TOUCHES.

1. Apply moisture-resistant glue to ⅜"-dia. wood plugs, and insert them into each counterbored screw hole. Sand the plugs flush with the wood.

2. Sand all surfaces smooth with medium (100- or 120-grit) sandpaper. Finish-sand with fine (150- or 180-grit) sandpaper.

3. Finish as desired—try two thin coats of primer and two coats of exterior house trim paint **(photo H).** Whenever you use untreated pine for an outdoor project, be sure to use an exterior-rated finish to protect the wood.

Trellis Planter

Two traditional yard furnishings are combined into one compact package.

The decorative trellis and the cedar planter are two staples found in many yards and gardens. By integrating the appealing shape and pattern of the trellis with the rustic, functional design of the cedar planter, this project showcases the best qualities of both furnishings.

Because the 2 × 2 lattice trellis is attached to the planter, not permanently fastened to a wall or railing, the trellis planter can be moved easily to follow changing sunlight patterns, or to occupy featured areas of your yard. It is also easy to move into storage during non-growing seasons. You may even want to consider installing wheels or casters on the base for greater mobility.

Building the trellis planter is a very simple job. The trellis portion is made entirely of strips of 2 × 2 cedar, fashioned together in a crosshatch pattern. The planter bin is a basic wood box, with panel sides and a two-board bottom with drainage holes, that rests on a scalloped base. The trellis is screwed permanently to the back of the planter bin.

Stocking the trellis planter with plantings is a matter of personal taste and growing conditions. In most areas, ivy, clematis and grapevines are good examples of climbing plants that can be trained up the trellis. Ask at your local gardening center for advice on plantings. Plants can be set into the bin in containers, or you can fill the bin with potting soil and plant directly in the bin.

CONSTRUCTION MATERIALS

Quantity	Lumber
1	2 × 6" × 8' cedar
1	2 × 4" × 6' cedar
4	2 × 2" × 8' cedar
3	1 × 6" × 8' cedar
1	1 × 2" × 6' cedar

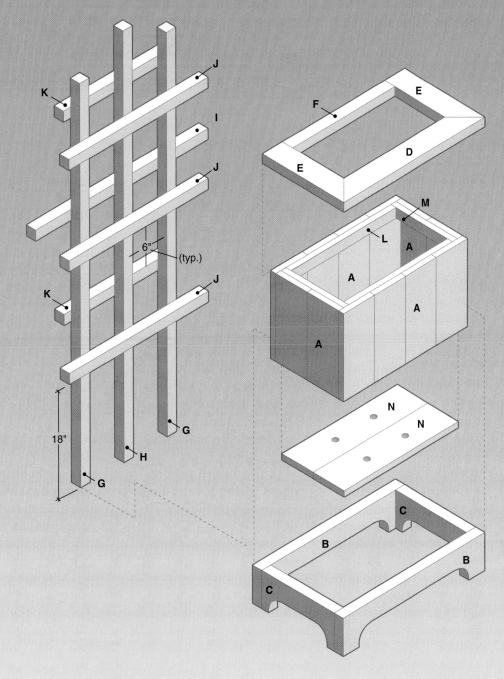

OVERALL SIZE:
69" HIGH
17¼" DEEP
30" LONG

6" (typ.)

18"

	Cutting List			
Key	**Part**	**Dimension**	**Pcs.**	**Material**
A	Box slat	⅞ × 5½ × 13"	12	Cedar
B	Base front/back	1½ × 5½ × 25"	2	Cedar
C	Base end	1½ × 5½ × 12¾"	2	Cedar
D	Cap front	1½ × 3½ × 25"	1	Cedar
E	Cap end	1½ × 3½ × 14¼"	2	Cedar
F	Cap back	1½ × 1½ × 18"	1	Cedar
G	End post	1½ × 1½ × 59½"	2	Cedar

	Cutting List			
Key	**Part**	**Dimension**	**Pcs.**	**Material**
H	Center post	1½ × 1½ × 63½"	1	Cedar
I	Long rail	1½ × 1½ × 30"	1	Cedar
J	Medium rail	1½ × 1½ × 24"	3	Cedar
K	Short rail	1½ × 1½ × 18"	2	Cedar
L	Cleat	⅞ × 1½ × 18½"	2	Cedar
M	Cleat	⅞ × 1½ × 11"	2	Cedar
N	Bottom board	⅞ × 5½ × 20¼"	2	Cedar

Materials: Moisture-resistant glue, #8 2" wood screws, 1⅝", 2½" deck screws, finishing materials.

Note: Measurements reflect the actual size of dimension lumber.

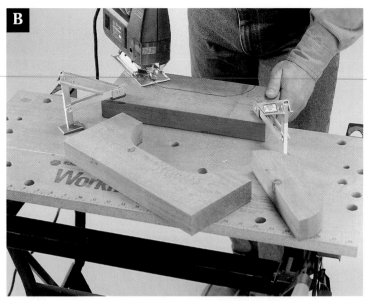

Attach the side cleats flush with the tops of the side boards.

Use a jig saw to make scalloped cutouts in all four base pieces—make sure the cutouts in matching pieces are the same.

Directions: Trellis Planter

BUILD THE PLANTER BIN.

1. Cut the box slats (A) and cleats (L, M) to length. Arrange the slats edge to edge in two groups of four and two groups of two, with tops and bottoms flush.

2. Center a long cleat (L) at the top of each set of four slats, so the distance from each end of the cleat to the end of the panel is the same. Attach the cleats to the four-slat panels by driving 1⅝" deck screws **(photo A)** through the cleats and into the slats.

3. Lay the short cleats (M) at the tops of the two-slat panels. Attach them to the slats the same way.

4. Arrange all four panels into a box shape and apply moisture-resistant wood glue to the joints. Attach the panels by driving 1⅝" deck screws through the four-slat panels and into the ends of the two-slat panels.

INSTALL THE BIN BOTTOM.

1. Cut the bottom boards (N) to length. Set the bin upside down on your work surface, and mark reference lines on the inside faces of the panels, ⅞" in from the bottom of the bin. Insert the bottom boards into the bin, aligned with the reference lines to create a ⅞" recess. Scraps of 1× cedar can be slipped beneath the bottom boards as spacers.

2. Drill ⅛" pilot holes through the panels. Counterbore the holes slightly with a counterbore bit. Fasten the bottom boards by driving 1⅝" deck screws through the panels, and into the edges and ends of the bottom boards.

BUILD THE PLANTER BASE.

The planter base is scalloped to create feet at the corners.

1. Cut the base front and back (B) and the base ends (C) to length. To draw the contours for the scallops on the front and back boards, set the point of a compass at the bottom edge of the base front, 5" in from one end. Set the compass to a 2½" radius, and draw a curve to mark the curved end of the cutout (see *Diagram*, page 135). Draw a straight line to connect the tops of the curves, 2½" up from the bottom of the board, to complete the scalloped cutout.

2. Make the cutout with a jig saw, then sand any rough spots in the cut. Use the board as a template for marking a matching cutout on the base back.

3. Draw a similar cutout on one base end, except with the point of the compass 3½" in from the ends. Cut out both end pieces with a jig saw **(photo B).**

4. Draw reference lines for wood screws, ¾" from the ends of the base front and back. Drill three evenly spaced pilot holes through the lines. Counterbore the holes. Fasten the base ends between the base front and back by driving three evenly spaced deck screws at each joint.

ATTACH THE BIN TO THE BASE.

1. Set the base frame and planter bin on their backs. Position the planter bin inside

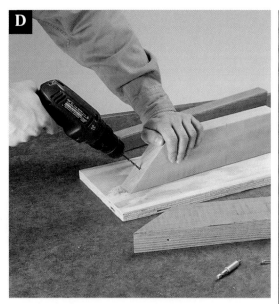

The recess beneath the bottom boards in the planter bin provides access for driving screws.

Before attaching the cap ends, drill pilot holes through the mitered ends of the cap front ends.

the base so it extends ⅞" past the top of the base.

2. Drive 1⅝" deck screws through the planter bin and into the base to secure the parts **(photo C).**

MAKE THE CAP FRAME.

1. Cut the cap front (D), cap ends (E) and cap back (F) to length. Cut 45° miters at one end of each cap end, and at both ends of the cap front.

2. Join the mitered corners by drilling pilot holes through the joints **(photo D).** Counterbore the holes. Fasten the pieces with glue and 2½" deck screws. Clamp the cap front and cap ends to the front of your worktable to hold them while you drive the screws.

3. Fasten the cap back between the cap ends with wood screws, making sure the back edges are flush. Set the cap frame on the planter bin so the back edges are flush. Drill pilot holes. Counterbore them. Drive 2½" deck screws through the cap frame and into the side and end cleats.

MAKE THE TRELLIS.

The trellis is made from pieces in a crosshatch pattern. The exact number and placement of the pieces is up to you—use the same spacing we used (see *Diagram),* or create your own.

1. Cut the end posts (G), center post (H) and rails (I, J, K) to length. Lay the end posts and center post together side by side with their bottom edges flush, so you can gang-mark the rail positions.

2. Use a square as a guide for drawing lines across all three posts, 18" up from the bottom. Draw the next line 7½" up from the first. Draw additional lines across the posts, spaced 7½" apart.

3. Cut two 7"-wide scrap blocks, and use them to separate the posts as you assemble the trellis. Attach the rails to the posts in the sequence shown in the *Diagram,* using 2½" screws **(photo E).** Alternate from the fronts to the backs of the posts when installing the rails.

APPLY FINISHING TOUCHES.

Fasten the trellis to the back of the planter bin so the bottoms of the posts rest on the top edge of the base. Drill pilot holes in the posts. Counterbore the holes. Drive 2½" deck screws through the posts and into the cap frame. With a 1"-dia. spade bit, drill a pair of drainage holes in each bottom board. Stain the project with an exterior wood stain.

Temporary spacers hold the posts in position while the trellis crossrails are attached.

PROJECT
POWER TOOLS

Trellis Seat

Spice up your patio or deck with this sheltered seating structure. Set it in a secluded corner to create a warm, inviting outdoor living space.

CONSTRUCTION MATERIALS

Quantity	Lumber
1	4 × 4" × 6' cedar
2	2 × 8" × 8' cedar
5	2 × 4" × 12' cedar
1	1 × 6" × 10' cedar
11	1 × 2" × 8' cedar
2	½" × 4 × 4' cedar lattice

Made of lattice and cedar boards, our trellis seat is ideal for conversation or quiet moments of reading. The lattice creates just the right amount of privacy for a small garden or patio. It's an unobtrusive structure that is sure to add some warmth to your patio or deck. Position some outdoor plants along the top cap or around the frame sides to dress up the project and bring nature a little closer to home. For a cleaner appearance, conceal visible screw heads on the seat by counterboring the pilot holes for the screws and inserting cedar plugs (available at most woodworking stores) into the counterbores.

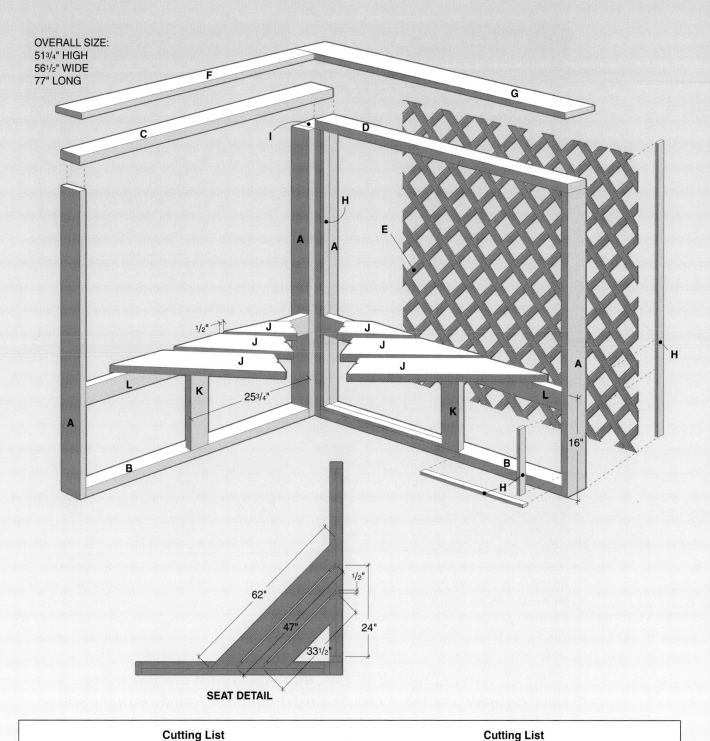

OVERALL SIZE:
51³/₄" HIGH
56½" WIDE
77" LONG

SEAT DETAIL

Cutting List

Key	Part	Dimension	Pcs.	Material
A	Frame side	1½ × 3½ × 49½"	4	Cedar
B	Frame bottom	1½ × 3½ × 48"	2	Cedar
C	Long rail	1½ × 3½ × 56½"	1	Cedar
D	Short rail	1½ × 3½ × 51"	1	Cedar
E	Lattice	½" × 4 × 4'	2	Cedar
F	Short cap	¾ × 5½ × 51"	1	Cedar

Cutting List

Key	Part	Dimension	Pcs.	Material
G	Long cap	¾ × 5½ × 56½"	1	Cedar
H	Retaining strip	¾ × 1½" cut to fit	22	Cedar
I	Post	3½ × 3½ × 49½"	1	Cedar
J	Seat board	1½ × 7¼ × *	3	Cedar
K	Brace	1½ × 3½ × 11"	2	Cedar
L	Seat support	1½ × 3½ × 48"	2	Cedar

Materials: Moisture-resistant glue, 1¼", 2", 2½" and 3" deck screws, 4d galvanized casing nails, finishing materials.

Note: Measurements reflect the actual size of dimension lumber. *Cut one each: 32", 49", 63"

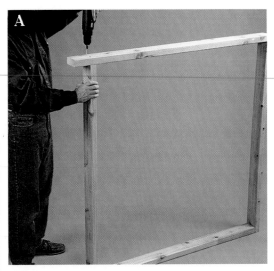

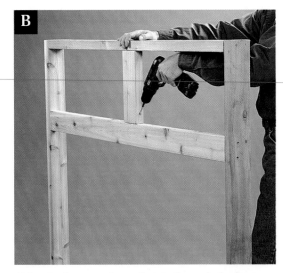

Attach the long rail at the top of one trellis frame with a 3½" overhang at one end to cover the post.

Drive deck screws toenail-style through the braces and into the seat supports.

Directions:
Trellis Seat

MAKE THE TRELLIS FRAME.
1. Cut the frame sides (A), frame bottoms (B), long rail (C), short rail (D), braces (K) and seat supports (L) to length. To attach the frame sides and frame bottoms, drill two evenly spaced ³⁄₁₆" pilot holes in the frame sides. Counterbore the holes ¼" deep, using a counterbore bit. Fasten with glue and drive 2½" deck screws through the frame sides and into the bottoms.
2. Drill pilot holes in the top faces of the long and short rails. Counterbore the holes. Attach the long and short rails to the tops of the frame sides with glue. Drive deck screws through the rails and into the ends of the frame sides. The

long rail should extend 3½" past one end of the frame **(photo A).**
3. Mark points 22¼" from each end on the frame bottoms to indicate position for the braces. Turn the frame upside-down. Drill pilot holes in the frame bottoms where the braces will be attached. Counterbore the holes. Position the braces flush with the inside frame bottom edges. Attach the pieces by driving 3" deck screws through the frame bottoms and into the ends of the braces.
4. Position the seat supports 16" up from the bottoms of the frame bottoms, resting on the braces. Make sure the supports are flush with the inside edges of the braces. Attach with glue and 3" deck screws driven through the frame sides and into the ends of the seat supports.

Fasten the trellis frames to the post at right angles.

5. Attach the braces to the seat supports by drilling angled ³⁄₁₆" pilot holes through each brace edge. Drive 3" deck screws toenail style through the braces and into the top edges of the seat supports **(photo B).**

JOIN THE TRELLIS FRAMES TO THE POST.
1. Cut the post (I) to length.
2. Attach the two frame sections to the post. First, drill pilot holes in the frame sides. Counterbore the holes. Drive evenly spaced 3" deck screws through the frame sides and into the

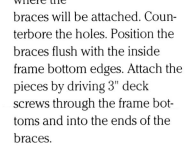

Nail 1 × 2 retaining strips for the lattice panels to the inside faces of the trellis frames.

Fasten the lattice panels to the seat supports with 1¼" deck screws, then attach outer retaining strips.

post **(photo C).** Make sure the overhang of the long rail fits snugly over the top of the post.

ATTACH THE LATTICE RETAINING STRIPS.

1. Cut the lattice retaining strips (H) to fit along the inside faces of the trellis frames (but not the seat supports or braces).
2. Nail the strips to the frames, flush with the inside frame edges, using 4d galvanized casing nails **(photo D).**

CUT AND INSTALL THE LATTICE PANELS.

1. Since you will probably be cutting through some metal fasteners in the lattice, fit your circular saw with a remodeler's blade. Sandwich the lattice panel between two boards near the cutting line to prevent the lattice from separating. Clamp the boards and the panel together, and cut the lattice panels to size. Always wear protective eyewear when operating power tools.
2. Position the panels into the frames against the retaining strips, and attach them to the seat supports with 1¼" deck

screws **(photo E).** Secure the panels by cutting retaining strips to fit along the outer edges of the inside faces of the trellis frame. Nail strips in place.

BUILD THE SEAT.

1. Cut the seat boards (J) to length. On a flat work surface, lay the seat boards together, edge to edge. Insert ½"-wide spacers between the boards.
2. Draw cutting lines to lay out the seat shape onto the boards as if they were one board (see *Seat Detail,* page 139, for seat board dimensions). Gang-cut the seat boards to their finished size and shape with a circular saw.
3. Attach the seat boards to the seat supports with evenly spaced deck screws, maintaining the ½"-wide gap. Smooth the seat board edges with a sander or router.

INSTALL THE TOP CAPS.

1. Cut the short cap (F) and long cap (G).
2. Attach the caps to the tops of the long and short rails with deck screws **(photo F).**

APPLY FINISHING TOUCHES.

Brush on a coat of clear wood sealer to help preserve the trellis seat.

Attach the long and short caps to the tops of the trellis frames. The long cap overlaps the long rail and the post.

Play Center

With this portable play center, children can have fun storing and organizing their toys right where they play with them.

CONSTRUCTION MATERIALS

Quantity	Lumber
1	¾" × 4 × 8' plywood
1	2 × 4" × 6' pine

Provide toddlers and young children with a clean, safe, easily accessible storage and play area with this efficient, portable play center. Built at heights that are comfortable for kids, the top shelves are meant to be used as play surfaces. They can even be fitted with plastic containers to hold sand, water, blocks or dolls. This unit is completely portable, so you can roll it onto the deck, put it under a favorite shade tree, or park it on the backyard patio. And if the weather isn't cooperating, you can bring it indoors to the family room. The play center is so simple to make, you may want to have the kids chip in and help you build it.

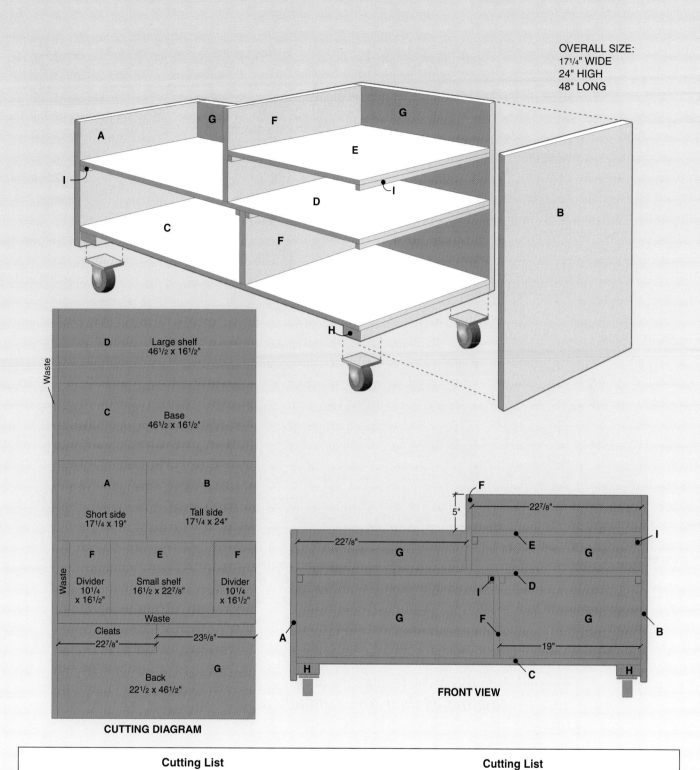

OVERALL SIZE:
17¼" WIDE
24" HIGH
48" LONG

CUTTING DIAGRAM

D — Large shelf 46½ x 16½"

C — Base 46½ x 16½"

Waste

A — Short side 17¼ x 19"

B — Tall side 17¼ x 24"

F — Divider 10¼ x 16½"

E — Small shelf 16½ x 22⅞"

F — Divider 10¼ x 16½"

Waste

Cleats 22⅞" — 23⅝"

Waste

Back 22½ x 46½" — G

FRONT VIEW

5"

22⅞"

22⅞"

19"

Cutting List

Key	Part	Dimension	Pcs.	Material
A	Short side	¾ × 17¼ × 19"	1	MDO plywood
B	Tall side	¾ × 17¼ × 24"	1	MDO plywood
C	Base	¾ × 16½ × 46½"	1	MDO plywood
D	Large shelf	¾ × 16½ × 46½"	1	MDO plywood
E	Small shelf	¾ × 16½ × 22⅞"	1	MDO plywood
F	Divider	¾ × 16½ × 10¼"	2	MDO plywood
G	Back	¾ × 23½ × 46½"	1	MDO plywood
H	Base cleat	1½ × 3½ × 16½"	2	Pine
I	Shelf cleat	¾ × ¾ × 16½"	6	MDO plywood

Materials: Moisture-resistant glue, 1¼" and 3" deck screws, tape measure, wood putty, finishing materials, locking casters (4).

Note: Measurements reflect the actual size of dimension lumber.

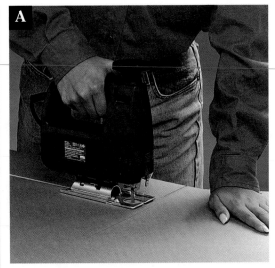

Use a jig saw to cut out a rectangular section of the back panel.

Attach cleats to the side panels at shelf locations.

Slip a divider between the base and the large shelf to support and compartmentalize the large shelf.

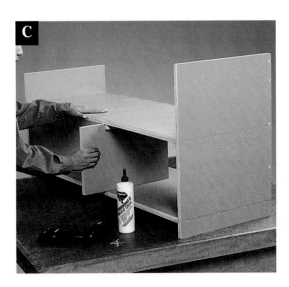

Directions: Play Center

CUT THE SIDES, BACK AND BASE.

1. Cut the short side (A), tall side (B), base (C) and back (G) to size (see *Cutting List,* page 143). Use a circular saw and a straightedge guide to cut plywood panels.
2. To cut the back into an L-shape, make layout lines for a rectangular cutout at one corner. Measure down 5" from the corner on the short side of the panel, and measure out 22⅞" on the long side of the panel. Extend the marks out onto the face of the panel, using a square. Cut out along the lines to the point of intersection, using a jig saw **(photo A).** Remove the rectangular cutout and sand the panel's edges.

ATTACH CLEATS TO PANELS.

1. Cut a long strip of plywood from a waste area (see *Cutting Diagram,* page 143). Cut the strip into six 16½"-long pieces to use as shelf cleats.
2. Mark reference lines at the shelf height on the short side and tall side panels. On the inside faces of each side panel, draw a straight line 13" up from the bottom edge to mark shelf-cleat height for the large shelf. Draw another straight line 5¾" down from the top of the tall side panel to mark the shelf-cleat height for the small shelf. Attach a cleat (I) to the panels just below each of these marks. Drill ⅛" pilot holes in each cleat. Counterbore the holes ¼" deep, using a counterbore bit. Attach the cleats with glue and drive 1¼" deck screws through the cleats and into the side panels **(photo B).**
3. Cut the base cleats (H) to length. Mark reference lines for the cleats 2" up from the bottom edge of each side panel. Drill pilot holes in the side panels just below the reference lines. Counterbore the holes. Attach the base cleats with glue and drive 3" deck screws through the outside faces of the side panels and into the edges of the cleats.

INSTALL THE BASE AND LARGE SHELF.

1. With the side panels propped in an upright position,

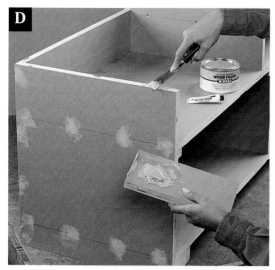

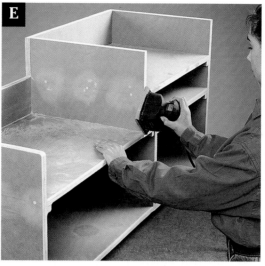

Fill screw holes and surface defects with exterior-rated wood filler or putty, then sand putty smooth.

Finish-sand the project with 220-grit sandpaper.

set the base onto the base cleats so it is flush with the insides and front edges of the panels.

2. Drill four pilot holes in the outside face of each side panel. Counterbore the holes. Attach the base with glue and drive 1¼" deck screws through the outside faces of the side panels and into the edges of the base.

3. Cut the large shelf (D) to size. Set it on the shelf cleats on each side panel, making sure the front of the shelf is flush with the fronts of the side panels. Drill pilot holes in the side panels. Counterbore the holes. Attach the shelf with glue and drive screws through the side panels and into the edges of the shelf.

ATTACH THE DIVIDERS.

1. Cut the dividers (F) to size. On one divider, mark a straight line 5¾" down from the top. Install a shelf cleat for the small shelf just below the line.

2. Glue two shelf cleats ¾" apart on the underside of the large shelf, centered around a mark 19" from the inside of the tall side panel. Once the glue dries,

insert the cleatless divider between the cleats on the shelf **(photo C).** Attach by driving 1¼" deck screws through the shelf and base and into the edges of the divider.

3. Attach the cleated divider to the top surface of the large shelf so the divider side with the cleat is 22⅞" away from the tall side panel.

4. Cut the small shelf (E) to size. Set it on the cleats on the top divider and the tall side panel. Attach with deck screws.

5. Position the back panel so it fits between the side panels, flush against the back edges of the shelves and dividers. Drill pilot holes where the back panel meets the shelves and dividers. Counterbore the holes and drive deck screws through the holes. Attach the side panels to the back panel in the same manner.

COMPLETE THE PLAY CENTER.

1. Fill screw holes and plywood voids with wood putty **(photo D).** Sand the putty until it is level with the surrounding surface **(photo E).** Finish-sand the entire project with 220-grit sandpaper.

2. Wipe off the sanding residue with a rag dipped in mineral spirits. Apply a coat of exterior primer. After the primer dries, paint the play center with exterior paint that dries to an enamel finish **(photo F).** Attach a locking caster near both ends of each base cleat.

Prime and paint all surfaces on the play center.

Boot Butler

A traditional piece of home furniture, the boot butler combines shoe storage and seating in one dependable unit.

CONSTRUCTION MATERIALS

Quantity	Lumber
1	¾" × 4 × 8' plywood
2	4" × 4' pine ranch molding

This boot butler was designed for an enclosed front porch, but it can be used near the entrance to your home or cabin. It provides plenty of storage space and gives you a place to sit when you're putting on or removing shoes and boots. It's a classic piece of household furniture modernized and simplified for your home.

To help keep things tidy and clean, just fit some plastic boot trays neatly onto the bottom shelf. When the trays get dirty, simply take them out and clean them. The boot butler can store footwear of the entire family. It fits conveniently against the wall to save space and keep unsightly boots and shoes out of busy traffic lanes.

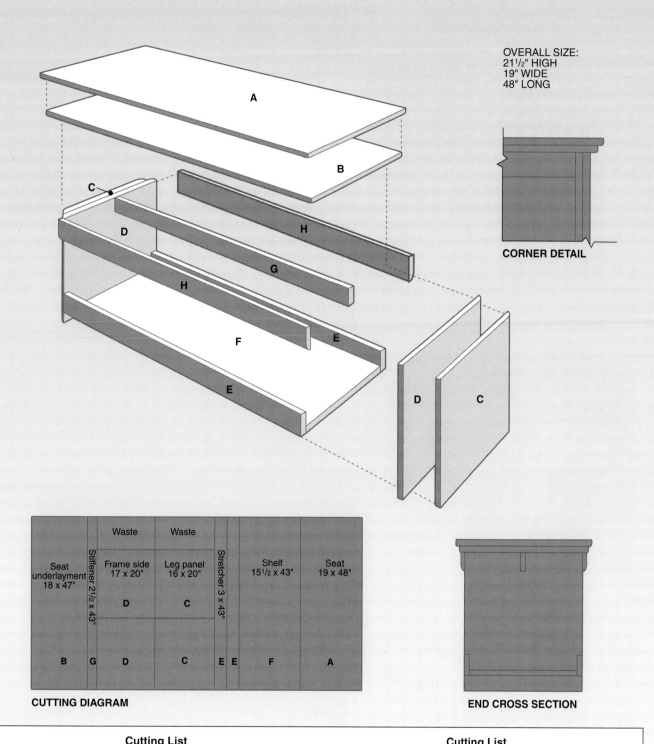

OVERALL SIZE:
21½" HIGH
19" WIDE
48" LONG

CORNER DETAIL

CUTTING DIAGRAM

Cutting diagram labels:
- Seat underlayment 18 x 47"
- Stiffener 2½ x 43"
- Waste — Frame side 17 x 20"
- Waste — Leg panel 16 x 20"
- Stretcher 3 x 43"
- Shelf 15½ x 43"
- Seat 19 x 48"
- B G D C E E F A

END CROSS SECTION

Cutting List				
Key	**Part**	**Dimension**	**Pcs.**	**Material**
A	Seat	¾ × 19 × 48"	1	Plywood
B	Underlayment	¾ × 18 × 47"	1	Plywood
C	Leg panel	¾ × 16 × 20"	2	Plywood
D	Frame side	¾ × 17 × 20"	2	Plywood

Cutting List				
Key	**Part**	**Dimension**	**Pcs.**	**Material**
E	Stretcher	¾ × 3 × 43"	2	Plywood
F	Shelf	¾ × 15½ × 43"	1	Plywood
G	Stiffener	¾ × 2½ × 43"	1	Plywood
H	Apron	½ × 3½ × 43¾"	2	Pine

Materials: Moisture-resistant glue, 1¼" and 2" deck screws, 8d finish nails, 15 × 21" plastic boot trays, finishing materials.

Note: Measurements reflect the actual size of dimension lumber.

Directions: Boot Butler

CUT THE PLYWOOD PARTS.

1. Cut the following parts with a circular saw and straightedge: seat (A), seat underlayment (B), leg panel (C), frame side (D), stretchers (E), shelf (F) and stiffener (G). Refer to the *Cutting Diagram* on page 147 to see how to cut all the parts from one sheet of plywood.

2. Smooth the sides and bottom edges of the legs, the top edges of the stretchers, and all the edges of the seat and underlayment with a sander or a router and ¼" roundover bit.

Use glue to reinforce the joints between the stretchers and the shelf.

ASSEMBLE THE SHELF AND STRETCHERS.

All the plywood parts are connected with screws and glue. Before you drive any screws, drill counterbores for the screw heads that are just deep enough to be filled with wood filler or putty.

1. Attach the stretchers (E) to the shelf (F) by drilling four evenly spaced ⅛" pilot holes through the outside edges of the stretchers and into the front and back edges of the shelf. Keep the screw holes at least 2" from the ends of the stretchers to prevent splitting.

2. Glue the joints **(photo A)**, and drive 2" deck screws through the pilot holes and into the shelf.

BUILD THE BOX FRAME.

1. Attach the two frame sides (D) to the ends of the shelf assembly. Begin by measuring and marking a line 2" up from the bottom edge of each frame side. The stretcher's lower edges will fit here.

2. Position the stiffener (G) between the frame sides at the top centerpoints. Mark the stiffener's position, making sure

the top of the stiffener is flush with the tops of the frame sides. Apply glue to all the joints.

3. Clamp the stretchers and stiffener in position with bar clamps. Drill two evenly spaced ⅛" pilot holes through each frame side and into the ends of the stiffener. Drive in 2" deck screws to secure the stiffener **(photo B).** For extra shelf support, drill pilot holes and drive a screw through the center of each frame side into the shelf.

COMPLETE THE LEG ASSEMBLY.

Attach leg panels (C) to the outer faces of the frame sides to provide wider, more stable support points for the seat.

1. Put wax paper or newspaper on your work surface to catch any excess glue. Apply glue to the outer face of each frame side and to the inner face of each leg panel. Press the leg panels against the frame panels, centered side to side to create a ½" reveal on each side of each frame panel. All top and bottom edges should be flush. Clamp each panel pair together **(photo C).**

The stiffener is screwed in place between the sides to keep the boot butler square.

A pair of plywood panels are fastened together to create each leg assembly.

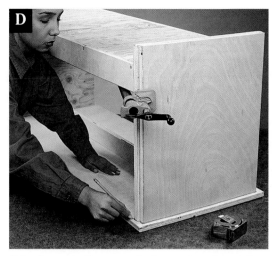

If the frame isn't square, fasten a pipe clamp diagonally across it and tighten.

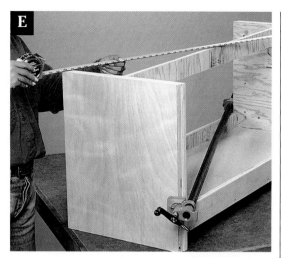

Set the frame assembly onto the underlayment. Center and trace the outline on the underlayment.

2. Drill pilot holes in the frame sides and counterbore the holes. Drive 1¼" deck screws through the frame sides and into the leg panels.

3. Measure the box frame diagonally from corner to corner, across the tops of the leg assembly to make sure it is square. Use a pipe clamp to draw the frame together until it is square and the diagonal measurements are equal **(photo D).**

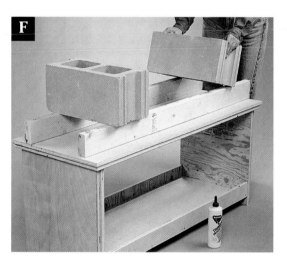

Apply weight on the seat to ensure a solid bond with the underlayment.

ATTACH THE SEAT.

The seat for the boot butler is made of an underlayment (B) layered with a plywood seat (A).

1. Lay the underlayment on a flat surface. Turn the leg and shelf assembly upside down and center it on the bottom face of the underlayment. Outline edges of the frame onto the underlayment **(photo E).**

2. Flip the leg and shelf assembly upright. Apply glue to the tops of the legs and stiffener. Position the underlayment on the assembly according to the alignment marks.

3. Drill ⅛" pilot holes through the underlayment into the legs and stiffeners. Counterbore the holes. Drive in 2" deck screws.

4. Apply a thin layer of glue to the top of the underlayment and the underside of the seat. Position the seat on the underlayment so the overhang is equal on all sides. Set heavy weights on top of the seat to create a solid glue bond **(photo F).**

5. Drill evenly spaced pilot holes in the underlayment and counterbore the holes. Drive 1¼" deck screws through the underlayment into the seat.

6. Cut the aprons (H) from 4"-wide pine ranch molding. Position them so the tops of the aprons are flush against the bottom edges of the underlayment, overlapping the edges of

the frame panels slightly. Attach them with 8d finish nails.

APPLY FINISHING TOUCHES.

1. Fill all of the counterbored screw holes and plywood edges with wood putty and sand smooth.

2. Apply primer and paint. For a decorative touch, stencil or sponge-paint the surfaces.

TIP

Rigid, clear plastic boot trays are sold at most discount stores or building centers. The Boot Butler project shown here is designed to hold 15 × 21" plastic boot trays.

PROJECT
POWER TOOLS

Tree Surround

*Turn wasted space beneath a mature tree
into a shady seating area.*

CONSTRUCTION MATERIALS

Quantity	Lumber
11	2 × 4" × 8' cedar
2	1 × 6" × 8' cedar
24	1 × 4" × 8' cedar

This tree surround with built-in benches provides ample seating in your yard, while protecting the base of the tree trunk. Situated in a naturally shady area, the surround/bench creates an ideal spot to relax with a good book or spend a quiet moment alone.

The tree surround can be built in four pieces in your garage or basement, then assembled on-site to wrap around the tree. As shown, the tree surround will fit a tree trunk up to 25" in diameter. But with some basic math, it's easy to adjust the sizes of the pieces so the surround fits just about any tree in your yard.

Unlike most tree bench designs, this project is essentially freestanding and does not require you to set posts (digging holes at the base of a tree can be next to impossible in some cases). And because it is cedar, it will blend right into most landscapes.

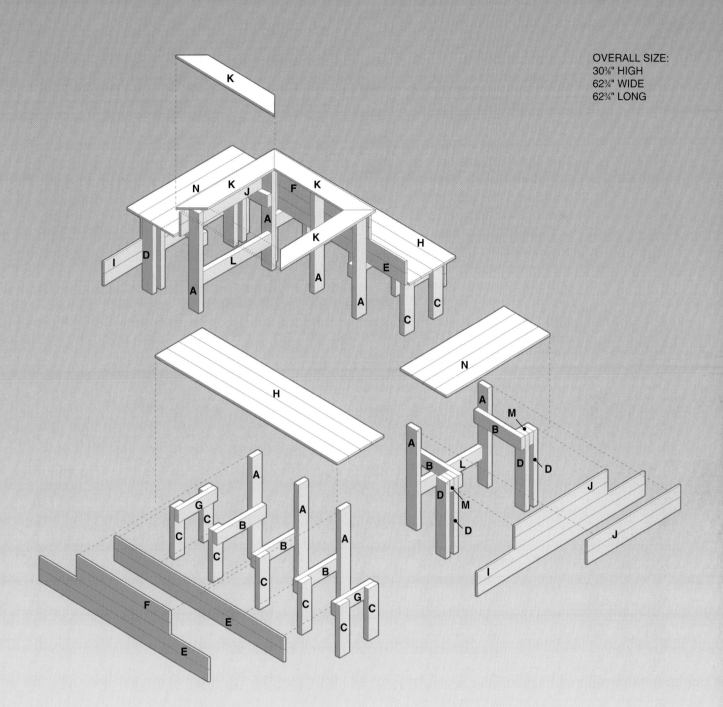

Cutting List

Key	Part	Dimension	Pcs.	Material
A	Inside post	1½ × 3½ × 29½"	10	Cedar
B	Seat rail	1½ × 3½ × 16¾"	10	Cedar
C	Short post	1½ × 3½ × 15"	14	Cedar
D	Long post	1½ × 3½ × 22¼"	8	Cedar
E	Face board	⅞ × 3½ × 60½"	8	Cedar
F	Face board	⅞ × 3½ × 34"	4	Cedar
G	Side seat rail	1½ × 3½ × 13¼"	4	Cedar

Cutting List

Key	Part	Dimension	Pcs.	Material
H	Bench slat	⅞ × 3½ × 62¾"	8	Cedar
I	Face board	⅞ × 3½ × 58¾"	4	Cedar
J	Face board	⅞ × 3½ × 32¼"	8	Cedar
K	End cap	⅞ × 5½ × 36"	4	Cedar
L	Stringer	1½ × 3½ × 22¼"	2	Cedar
M	Nailer	1½ × 3½ × 3½"	4	Cedar
N	Bench slat	⅞ × 3½ × 36¼"	8	Cedar

Materials: Moisture-resistant glue, 1½" and 2½" deck screws, finishing materials.

Note: Measurements reflect the actual size of dimension lumber.

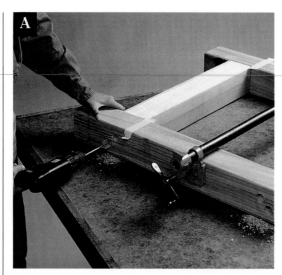

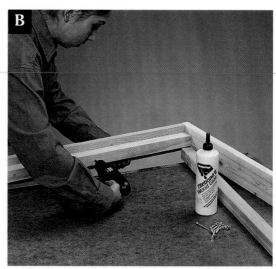

Counterbore two sets of holes on each leg to recess the lag bolts when you attach the legs to the stretchers.

Maintain a ¾" distance from the top edge of the rails to the top edge of the cleats.

Directions: Patio Table

PREPARE THE LEG ASSEMBLY.

1. Cut the legs (A), stretchers (B) and spreader (C) to length. Measure and mark 4" up from the bottom edge of each leg to mark the positions of the bottom edges of the lower stretchers.
2. Test-fit the legs and stretchers to make sure they are square. The top stretchers should be flush with the top leg ends.
3. Carefully position the pieces and clamp them together with pipe clamps. The metal jaws on the pipe clamps can damage the wood, so use protective clamping pads.

> ### TIP
> Buy or make wood plugs to fill screw holes and conceal screw heads. Building centers and woodworker's stores usually carry a variety of plug types in several sizes and styles. To cut your own wood plug, you can either use a special-purpose plug-cutting tool (sold at woodworker's stores), or a small hole saw that mounts to your power drill (sold at building centers). The diameter of the plug must match the counterbore drilled into the wood.

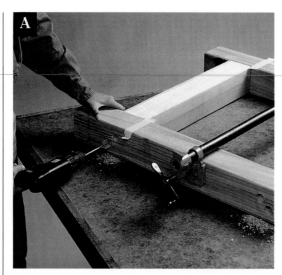

Use pencils or dowels to set even gaps between top slats. Tape slats in position with masking tape.

BUILD THE LEG ASSEMBLY.

1. Drill ⅞"-× ⅜"-deep counterbores positioned diagonally across the bottom end of each leg and opposite the lower stretchers **(photo A)**. Drill ¼" pilot holes through the counterbores and into the stretchers.
2. Unclamp the pieces and drill ⅜" holes for lag screws through the legs, using the pilot holes as center marks.
3. Apply moisture-resistant glue to the ends of the stretchers. Attach the legs to the stretchers

by driving lag screws with washers through the legs and into the stretchers. Use the same procedure to attach the spreader to the stretchers.

ATTACH CLEATS AND RAILS.

1. Cut the side rails (G) and end rails (H) to length. Drill two evenly spaced, ⅛" pilot holes through the ends of the side rails. Counterbore the holes ¼" deep, using a counterbore bit. Apply glue and fasten the side rails to the end rails

Directions:
Tree Surround

BUILD THE SHORT BENCH FRAMES.

The tree surround is built as two short benches on the sides, and two taller benches on the ends. The benches are joined together to wrap around the tree. Drill a ⅛" pilot hole for every screw used in this project. Counterbore the holes to a ¼" depth, using a counterbore bit.

1. To build the support frames for the short benches, cut the inside posts (A), seat rails (B) and short posts (C) to length. Lay a short post on top of an inside post, with the bottom ends flush. Trace a reference line onto the face of the inside post, following the top of the short post.

2. Separate the posts. Lay a seat rail across the faces of the two posts so it is flush with the outside edge and top of the short post, and just below the reference line on the inside post.

Use a square to make sure the seat rails are perpendicular to the posts and their ends are flush with the post edges. Join the pieces with moisture-resistant glue. Drive 2½" deck screws through the seat rails and into the short posts and inside posts. Make six of these assemblies **(photo A).**

3. Cut the four side seat rails (G) to length. Attach them to pairs of short posts so the tops and ends are flush.

TIP

Leave room for the tree to grow in trunk diameter when you build and install a tree surround. Allow at least 3" between the tree and the surround on all sides. Adjust the dimensions of your tree surround, if needed, to create the additional space.

Seat rails are attached to the short posts and inside posts to make the bench frames.

The face boards attached at the fronts of the short posts on the short benches should extend ⅞" past the edges of the posts.

ATTACH THE SHORT BENCH FACE BOARDS.

1. Cut the face boards (E) to length for the fronts of the short benches. Draw lines on the inside faces of these face boards, ⅞" and 14⅞" from each end, and at their centers. These reference lines will serve as guides when you attach the face boards to the short bench frames.

2. Lay the two frames made with two short posts on your work surface, with the back edges of the back posts down. Attach a face board to the front edges of the front posts, with 1½" deck screws, so the ends of the face board extend ⅞" be-

Attach face boards to the inside posts to create the backrest. The lowest board should be ⅛" above the seat rails.

TIP

Cover the ground at the base of a tree with a layer of landscaping stone or wood bark before you install a tree surround. To prevent weeds from growing up through the ground cover, lay landscaping fabric in the area first. Add a border of landscape edging to keep everything contained. If the ground at the base of the tree is not level, you can make installation of the tree surround easier by laying a base of landscaping rock, then raking it and tamping it until it is level.

yond the outside edges of the frames (the seat rail should be on the inside of the frame). Attach another face board ⅛" below the top face board, making sure the reference lines are aligned **(photo B).**

ASSEMBLE THE SHORT BENCHES.

1. Stand the frame and face board assemblies on their feet. Fit the short bench frames made with the inside posts against the inside faces of the face boards. Center the short posts of the frames on the reference lines drawn on the face boards. Attach these frames to the face boards with 1½" deck screws.

2. Set another face board at the backs of the seat rails, against the inside posts. Slip a 10d finish nail under the face board where it crosses each seat rail to create a ⅛" gap. Make sure the ends of the face board extend ⅞" beyond the edges of the end frames. Attach the face board to the inside posts with 1½" deck screws **(photo C).** Attach another face board ⅛" up

on the inside posts.

3. Cut the face boards (F) to length. Fasten two of these shorter face boards to each bench assembly so the ends overhang the inside posts by ⅞". Maintain a ⅛" gap between the face boards. The top edge of the highest face board on each bench assembly should be flush with the tops of the inside posts.

4. Cut the bench slats (H) to length. Position the front bench slat so it overhangs the front of the face board below it by 1⅛" and both ends of the face board by 1⅛" **(photo D).** Attach the front slat by driving two 1½" deck screws through the slat and into each seat rail. Fasten the back seat slat so it butts against the inside posts. Attach the remaining bench slats so the spaces between the slats are even.

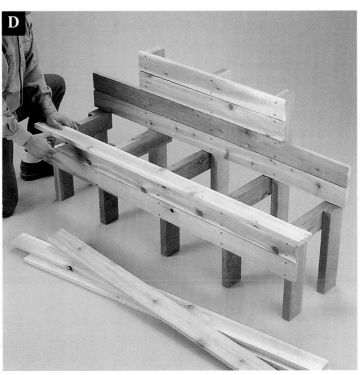

Measure to make sure the front bench slat overhangs the face board below it by 1⅛".

MAKE THE TALL BENCHES.
The two tall benches are built much like the short benches, but with doubled posts at the front, for extra strength, and a stringer to support the frames.

1. Cut the long posts (D) and four nailers (M) to length. Arrange the long posts in pairs, with nailers in between at the tops. Fasten the doubled posts and nailers together with glue and 2½" deck screws, making sure the nailers are aligned with the fronts and tops of the posts.

2. Attach a seat rail to the doubled posts **(photo E).** Then, attach the free end of each seat rail to an inside post, as you did for the short benches.

3. Cut the stringers (L) to length. Position a stringer between each pair of inside posts, flush with the back edges and 8" up from the bottoms of the posts. Attach them with glue and 2½" deck screws driven through the inside posts and into the ends of the stringers.

4. Cut the face boards for the tall benches (I, J) to length. Use 10d finish nails to leave ⅛" gaps between the face boards, as before, including the gap above the back ends of the seat rails. Use 1½" deck screws to attach two of the shorter boards (J) to the long posts so the top board is flush with the tops of the posts and seat rails, and the ends overhang the outside edges of the doubled posts by ½" **(photo F).**

5. Attach the longer face boards (I) below the shorter face boards, so they overhang the doubled posts by the same amount on each end **(photo G).** The overhang portions will

After making doubled posts for the tall benches, attach the seat rails.

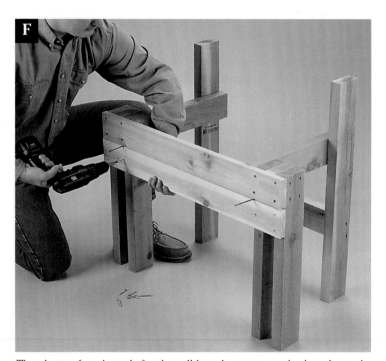

The shorter face boards for the tall benches are attached so the ends are flush with the outsides of the doubled posts.

cover the sides of the short bench frames after assembly. Attach two of the shorter face boards (J) to the front edges of the inside posts so their ends overhang the outside faces of the posts by 3½".

6. Cut the bench slats for the tall benches (N) to length. Position the slats on the seat rails. Fasten the front slat so it overhangs the front of the face board below it by 1⅛" and the ends of the face board by 2".

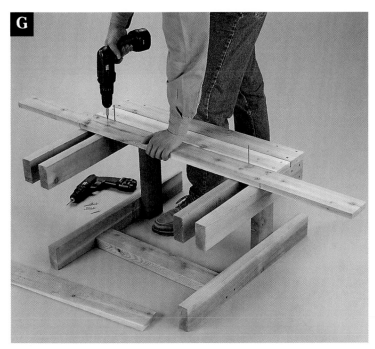

The longer face boards attached to the tall benches overhang the doubled posts so they cover the sides of the short bench frames when the tree surround is assembled.

Fasten a slat flush with the back of the bench. Attach the remaining slats on each tall bench so the spaces between the slats are even.

APPLY THE FINISH.
Now is a good time to apply a finish to the benches. Sand all the surfaces smooth and wipe the wood clean. Apply at least two coats of exterior wood stain to protect the wood.

ASSEMBLE THE TREE SURROUND.
1. If necessary, prepare the ground around the tree where the tree surround will stand (see *Tip Box,* page 85). When the ground is roughly level, you can assemble the tree surround and shim beneath the posts to level it.
2. Set all four benches around the tree so the overhang on the tall bench face boards covers the end frames of the short benches. The ends of the face boards should butt against the backs of the face boards on the short benches. Clamp or tack the benches together. Don't fasten the pieces together until you've made adjustments to level the tree surround.
3. Use a carpenter's level to check the tree surround. Set the level on each of the benches to determine whether adjustments are needed. For shims, use flat stones, such as flagstone, or prefabricated concrete pavers. If you don't want to use shims, mark the spots on the ground that need rais-ing or lowering, and separate the benches to make the required adjustments.
4. When the tree surround is level and the benches fit together squarely, attach the tall benches to the short benches by driving 2½" deck screws through the face boards on the tall benches and into the posts on the short benches.

ATTACH THE CAP.
1. Cut the end caps (K) to length. Draw 45° miter lines at each end of one cap, with both miter lines pointing inward. Make the miter cuts with a circular saw **(photo H)** or—even better—a power miter box.
2. Tack or clamp the end cap in place. Mark and cut the three remaining end caps one at a time to ensure even joints. Attach the caps with 1½" deck screws driven through the caps and into the ends of the inside posts. Sand the parts smooth and apply the same finish to the caps that you applied to the tree surround benches.

The 1 × 6 caps are mitered to make a square frame around the top of the tree surround after it is assembled around your tree.

Patio Table

*This patio table blends sturdy construction with rugged style
to offer many years of steady service.*

CONSTRUCTION MATERIALS

Quantity	Lumber
2	4 × 4" × 10' cedar
3	2 × 2" × 8' cedar
2	1 × 4" × 8' cedar
4	1 × 6" × 8' cedar

Everyone knows that a shaky, unstable patio table is a real headache. But you won't be concerned about wobbly legs with this patio table. It's designed for sturdiness and style. As a result, it's a welcome addition to any backyard patio or deck.

This all-cedar patio table is roomy enough to seat six, and strong enough to support a large patio umbrella—even in high wind. The legs and cross braces are cut from solid 4 × 4 cedar posts, then lag-bolted together. If you can find it at your local building center, buy heartwood cedar posts. Heartwood, cut from the center of the tree, is valued for its density, straightness and resistance to decay. Because it's used for an eating surface, you'll want to apply a natural, clear linseed-oil finish.

OVERALL SIZE:
28" HIGH
41½" WIDE
48" LONG

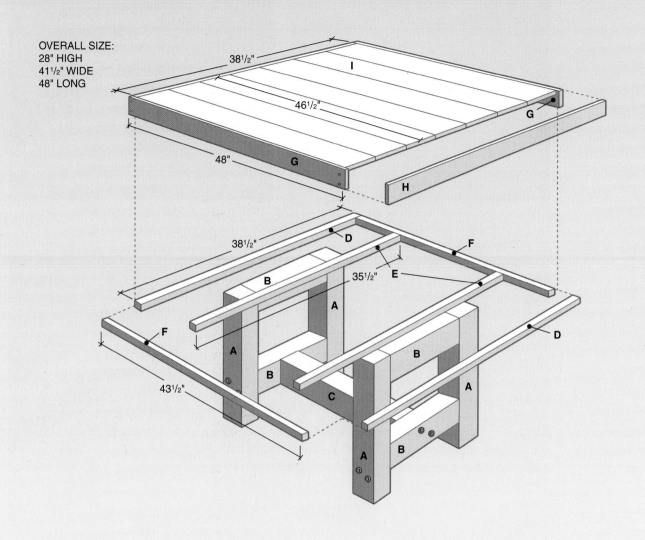

Cutting List						Cutting List				
Key	**Part**	**Dimension**	**Pcs.**	**Material**		**Key**	**Part**	**Dimension**	**Pcs.**	**Material**
A	Leg	3½ × 3½ × 27¼"	4	Cedar		**F**	Side cleat	1½ × 1½ × 43½"	2	Cedar
B	Stretcher	3½ × 3½ × 20"	4	Cedar		**G**	Side rail	¾ × 3½ × 48"	2	Cedar
C	Spreader	3½ × 3½ × 28"	1	Cedar		**H**	End rail	¾ × 3½ × 40"	2	Cedar
D	End cleat	1½ × 1½ × 40"	2	Cedar		**I**	Top slat	¾ × 5½ × 46½"	7	Cedar
E	Cross cleat	1½ × 1½ × 37"	2	Cedar						

Materials: Moisture-resistant glue, 2" and 3" deck screws, ⅜ × 6" lag screws with washers (20), finishing materials.

Note: Measurements reflect the actual size of dimension lumber.

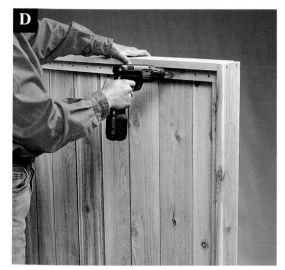

Fasten cross cleats to the tabletop for strength, and to provide an anchor for the leg assembly.

Keep a firm grip on the tabletop slats when drilling deck screws through the cleats.

Before you stain or treat the patio table, sand the surfaces smooth.

with 2" deck screws.

2. Cut the end cleats (D), cross cleats (E) and side cleats (F) to length. Fasten the end cleats to the end rails ¾" below the top edges of the rails with glue and 2" deck screws **(photo B).** Repeat this procedure with the side cleats and side rails.

CUT AND ATTACH THE TOP SLATS.

1. Cut the top slats (I) to length. Lay the slats into the tabletop frame so they rest on the cleats.

Carefully spread the slats apart so they are evenly spaced. Use masking tape to hold the slats in place once you achieve the correct spacing **(photo C).**

2. Stand the tabletop frame on one end and fasten the top slats in place by driving two 2" deck screws through the end cleats and into each slat **(photo D).** Hold or clamp each slat firmly while fastening to prevent the screws from pushing the slats away from the frame.

CONNECT THE LEGS AND TOP.

1. Turn the tabletop over and center the legs on the underside. Make sure the legs are the same distance apart at the top as they are at the bottom.

2. Lay the cross cleats along the insides of the table legs. Fasten the cross cleats to the tabletop with 2" deck screws **(photo E).** Fasten the cross cleats to the legs with 3" deck screws.

APPLY FINISHING TOUCHES.

1. For a more finished appearance, fill exposed screw holes with cedar plugs or buttons (see *Tip,* page 158). Smooth the edges of the table and legs with a sander or router **(photo F).**

2. If you want to fit the table with a patio umbrella, use a 1½"-dia. hole saw to cut a hole into the center of the tabletop. Use a drill and spade bit to cut the 1½"-dia. hole through the spreader.

3. Finish the table as desired—use clear linseed oil for a natural, nontoxic, protective finish.

Index